Cambridge Elements

Elements in Global China
edited by
Ching Kwan Lee
University of California-Los Angeles

CHINA FOR AFRICA'S INDUSTRIALIZATION?

Carlos Oya
SOAS University of London

Shaftesbury Road, Cambridge CB2 8EA, United Kingdom

One Liberty Plaza, 20th Floor, New York, NY 10006, USA

477 Williamstown Road, Port Melbourne, VIC 3207, Australia

314–321, 3rd Floor, Plot 3, Splendor Forum, Jasola District Centre, New Delhi – 110025, India

103 Penang Road, #05–06/07, Visioncrest Commercial, Singapore 238467

Cambridge University Press is part of Cambridge University Press & Assessment, a department of the University of Cambridge.

We share the University's mission to contribute to society through the pursuit of education, learning and research at the highest international levels of excellence.

www.cambridge.org
Information on this title: www.cambridge.org/9781009670968

DOI: 10.1017/9781009347679

© Carlos Oya 2025

This publication is in copyright. Subject to statutory exception and to the provisions of relevant collective licensing agreements, with the exception of the Creative Commons version the link for which is provided below, no reproduction of any part may take place without the written permission of Cambridge University Press & Assessment.

An online version of this work is published at doi.org/10.1017/9781009347679 under a Creative Commons Open Access license CC-BY-NC-ND 4.0 which permits re-use, distribution and reproduction in any medium for non-commercial purposes providing appropriate credit to the original work is given. You may not distribute derivative works without permission. To view a copy of this license, visit https://creativecommons.org/licenses/by-nc-nd/4.0

When citing this work, please include a reference to the DOI 10.1017/9781009347679

First published 2025

A catalogue record for this publication is available from the British Library

ISBN 978-1-009-67096-8 Hardback
ISBN 978-1-009-34769-3 Paperback
ISSN 2632-7341 (online)
ISSN 2632-7333 (print)

Cambridge University Press & Assessment has no responsibility for the persistence or accuracy of URLs for external or third-party internet websites referred to in this publication and does not guarantee that any content on such websites is, or will remain, accurate or appropriate.

For EU product safety concerns, contact us at Calle de José Abascal, 56, 1°, 28003 Madrid, Spain, or email eugpsr@cambridge.org

China for Africa's Industrialization?

Elements in Global China

DOI: 10.1017/9781009347679
First published online: November 2025

Carlos Oya
SOAS University of London

Author for correspondence: Carlos Oya, co2@soas.ac.uk

Abstract: China's engagement in Africa since 2000 consists of a diverse set of institutions, activities, relations, investment flows, and other economic statecraft events. These have generated opportunities for economic transformation, reviving the prospects for industrialization and job creation in some African countries following decades of neglect. While the case for industrialization-led structural transformation is strong, the proposed means of pursuing this pathway vary, necessitating bold vision and interventions. Whether through infrastructure funding and building, or direct greenfield investments, China is helping lay the foundations for industrialization in Africa, albeit unevenly and slowly. The vectors and outcomes are, however, variegated, calling for a comparative examination. Therefore, the Element illustrates variations in outcomes and the importance of context when considering the vectors of Africa–China engagements, how they contribute to industrialization prospects, and the central role of policy agency, bargaining, and contestation. This title is also available as Open Access on Cambridge Core.

Keywords: Global China, Africa–China relations, industrialization, political economy of development, employment

© Carlos Oya 2025

ISBNs: 9781009670968 (HB), 9781009347693 (PB), 9781009347679 (OC)
ISSNs: 2632-7341 (online), 2632-7333 (print)

Contents

1 Africa's Aspirations to Industrialize and the Role of China: Questions and Premises   1

2 China's Engagements in Africa Supporting Industrial Development   11

3 Chinese Firms, Economic Transformation, and Labour Dynamics: Building an Industrial Workforce in Africa   42

4 Policy, Politics, and Agency: Mediating the Impact of China on Africa's Industrialization   55

   List of Abbreviations   74

   References   75

1 Africa's Aspirations to Industrialize and the Role of China: Questions and Premises

Since the early 2000s, Chinese engagements in Africa[1] have grown at an unprecedented rate. Trade has expanded from $10bn in 2000 to $262bn in 2023, making China Africa's largest partner.[2] Meanwhile, China's foreign direct investment (FDI) stock in Africa has grown from $500mn in 2003 to over $40bn in 2023, reaching a peak of $46bn in 2018. Chinese funding for infrastructure and the contract revenues of Chinese construction companies in Africa have also risen many times over. These developments have coincided with a rollercoaster of macroeconomic trends in African countries, from the commodity boom of the 2000s to the effects of the global financial crisis, from the expansion in debt to the ravages of the COVID-19 pandemic. Driven by these contradictory forces, African economies have shown wide variations in economic performance, although the pending task of structural economic transformation looms large across most of the continent.

Only a very small number of African countries have managed to achieve a significant degree of industrialization. Nevertheless, recent years have seen a revival of industrialization aspirations, partly driven by Asian success stories and partly by growing discontent at the Western aid-led focus on market liberalization and 'good governance' reforms. This revival has been supported by the leverage and strategic 'triangulation' that China's growing engagement in Africa has offered (Large 2021). There are important historical antecedents in the postcolonial period for China's presence in Africa's infrastructure and manufacturing development, such as the large import-substituting West Africa Textiles investments in Nigeria or the famous Tazara Railway connecting Zambia and Tanzania (Sun 2017; Shinn 2019). What has changed, however, is the scale of China's engagement and its unprecedented growth. This multifaceted phenomenon has recently been analysed through the conceptual lens of 'Global China'. According to Lee (2022) and Franceschini and Loubere (2022), 'Global China' can be defined in different ways depending on the focus of analysis: as a policy framework; as a power project consisting of economic statecraft, patron–client relations and symbolic domination; or as a method of analysis for understanding China's globalization and its various manifestations. As such, 'Global China' consists of multiple actors with varying interests

---

[1] This Element employs the convention of using the term 'Africa' to refer mainly to sub-Saharan Africa (SSA). However, where statistics on China–Africa relations include North African countries, this will be flagged. There may also be specific references to some North African countries, especially Egypt, where China's role in supporting industrialization features in some of the relevant literature.
[2] www.sais-cari.org/data-china-africa-trade

(Taylor 2019), sometimes in fierce competition with one another, and always subject to bargaining and contestation from a variety of African state and non-state actors.

This is not the first time questions concerning China's impact on Africa's industrialization have been posed. As noted by Wolf (2016), there is a narrative contrast between: (a) studies (e.g. Kaplinsky 2008) emphasizing the negative impacts of China's engagement on Africa's manufacturing due to a flood of cheap imports affecting local manufacturers, especially after African markets liberalized since the 1980s and China joined the WTO in 2001; and (b) research focusing on the opportunities China's industrial upgrading generates for FDI-led light manufacturing development in Africa, as Chinese manufacturers move overseas (Lin 2018; Geda et al. 2018; Calabrese and Tang 2023). The former, pessimistic, view is influenced by the reality that Africa's manufacturing lacks competitive advantage vis-à-vis Asian exporters (not just China), and remains overly exposed to competition given the very liberal trade regimes prevalent in most African countries since the structural adjustment programmes (SAPs) of the 1980s. By contrast, more realist, optimistic accounts apply Hirschman's 'possibilist' lens and historical evidence that countries can develop productive capabilities against the odds, overcoming obstacles and pain (Cramer et al. 2020). But is industrialization really desirable or feasible in Africa? And how can be achieved?

1.1 Industrialization in Africa: Why, How, Where, and When?

There are various arguments promoting Africa's structural transformation, with the point of contention generally around which path to take and whether industrialization is a necessary component. Here, one initial question to ask is: Why industrialize? Desirability does not necessarily imply viability, however – structural transformation needs to be built, often over extended periods of time and in the face of various obstacles, which leads to a second question: How best to industrialize? These interrelated questions have spawned an extensive literature, summarized next. In doing so, the Element draws on the work of selected political economists working on structural change and industrialization in low- and middle-income countries (LMICs), including Hirschman, Amsden, Chang, and, more recently, Cramer et al. (2020), Hauge (2023), and Whittaker et al. (2020). These authors defend the 'art of the possible', arguing that even lowest-income countries can aspire to industrialize based on the previous experiences of early and late developers, the opportunities they seized, and the panoply of industrial policy tools they deployed. While lessons from the past are critical, important shifts (e.g. climate change, new geopolitical shocks, technological change) that may have created context-specific opportunities to leapfrog stages of structural transformation must also be taken into account.

There are two relevant sets of classic arguments arising from a heterodox development economics tradition. First are the 'Kaldor laws', which refer to the symbiotic relationship between manufacturing growth and scaling up on the one hand, and economy-wide productivity growth on the other. This is driven by increasing returns to scale in manufacturing, as well as the sector's particular properties, which make it a hub for technological change (in terms of both innovation and diffusion). These 'laws' have been repeatedly tested by empirical work applied to different country samples and time periods, demonstrating there is indeed a symbiotic relationship between manufacturing development and sustained economic and productivity growth (Thirlwall 2013; Hauge 2023; Cramer et al. 2020).

Second, Hirschman's work expands on manufacturing's strong growth and transformative properties by stressing the strong productive linkages – both backward and forward – generated in other sectors, such as cotton for textiles, business services and logistics, and multiple intra-industrial linkages that contribute to the expansion of industrial eco-systems (Hirschman 1958). In short, the development of manufacturing capabilities generates demand, new markets and technological opportunities for various other economic activities, from agriculture to transport to trade to other modern services.

Employment matters too, especially for countries experiencing population growth and a youth bulge, as is the case across much of Africa. Thus, if the Kaldor laws and Hirschman's productive linkages hold, industrialization can also be an engine for the mass creation of direct, indirect and induced jobs. As argued by Amsden (2012), only the emergence of larger-scale, more technologically capable employers able to make long-term investments supportive of mass job creation can help African workers escape the trap of risky, low-return self-employment. Here, the employment multiplier effect of manufacturing is very high, as every new job in the sector holds the potential for 3–4 additional jobs being created elsewhere in the economy as an indirect outcome (Cramer et al. 2020, 101).

Another relevant argument is that more diversified, industrial-led export growth – buttressed by inter-sector linkages – can contribute to a relaxing of balance-of-payments constraints, which for many low-income countries (LICs) are a key impediment to growth (Thirlwall 2013). More foreign exchange availability can in turn facilitate further structural transformation into other higher-value added sectors (Cramer et al. 2020).

Despite growing doubts over the viability of industrial-led transformation, and despite consideration being given to services acting as a 'substitute' (Rodrik and Sandhu 2024), the available evidence for the current era of so-called 'premature deindustrialization' (Rodrik 2016) suggests that manufacturing production and employment have actually continued to expand globally. Here, it should be noted that although the manufacturing's global employment *share* has not significantly changed (Haraguchi et al. 2017), the sector continues to attract a large and growing share of greenfield FDI (UNCTAD 2024). Moreover, even labour-intensive manufacturing exports have experienced rapid growth since 2000 (Figure 1; Kruse et al. 2023). This is even considering the fact that sector classifications fail to fully recognize the significance of manufacturing, given how much of what counts as 'services' is deeply connected to industrial production worldwide (Hauge 2023; Cramer et al. 2020). Thus, despite the rapid growth of services across different country income categories, manufacturing is far from a stagnant or declining sector. It is also clear – hence some of the pessimism in both high-income countries (HICs) and LICs – that there has been a reconfiguration of global manufacturing output, with China growing its share continuously, together with several other fast-industrializing Asian countries (Hauge 2023; UNIDO 2024).

A report by the World Bank (2021) argues that African countries currently enjoy favourable conditions to participate through manufacturing global value chains (GVCs), potentially giving them a window to industrialize faster. Hauge

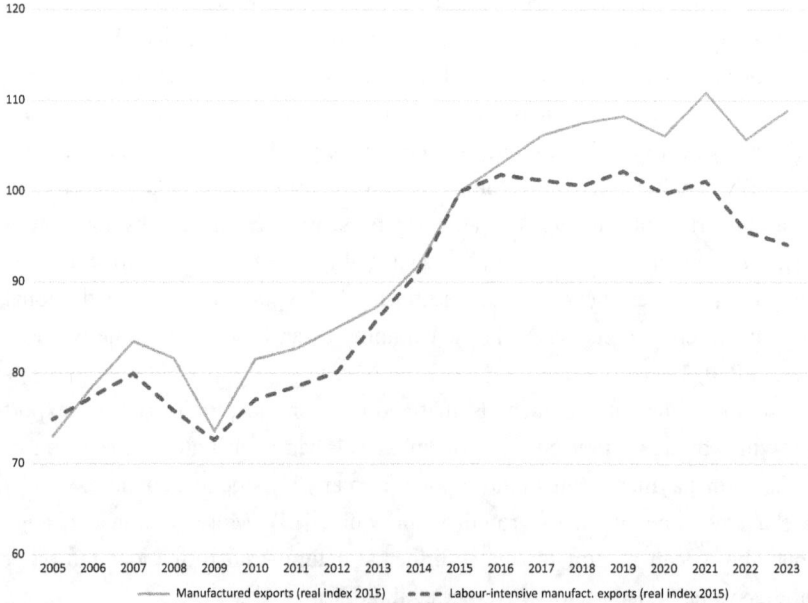

Figure 1 World manufactured exports 2005–2023

Source: Own elaboration from UNCTAD datasets

(2023) corroborates this with evidence of a growing number of countries entering manufacturing GVCs despite pressures for reshoring, mostly in Asia but also gradually in Africa. Thus, the fact that China is expected to increase its share of global manufacturing output (UNIDO 2024) does not preclude the possibility of African countries expanding their industrial output, especially in sectors deemed obsolete or no longer viable in Asian countries – China included – which are rapidly upgrading to high-tech manufacturing exports. Moreover, African countries, especially those with large markets, can potentially expand their industrial production through import substitution, a strategy many other economies have pursued in the past and are still trying now.

Any structural transformation strategy can and should learn from past successes and failures (Oqubay 2020). Historically, three stylized categories of industrializers can be identified. First, the experience of early industrializers such as Britain, which involved at least three interacting dominant factors (Allen 2011): (a) the availability of a new form of cheap energy (coal) making energy-intensive production units viable; (b) processes of social change driven by enclosures driving the formation of a proletariat available to work in new factories at subsistence wages; and (c) the availability of cheap raw materials, primarily cotton for the textile industry, facilitated by British imperialism and slavery in the cotton-growing American South (Inikori 2020).

Second, the experience of late industrializers in Asia in the post–World War II period, where another recipe with distinct ingredients arose: (a) the rise of a developmental state, driven by the imperatives of regime survival in the context of the Cold War; (b) the absence of a powerful landlord class, which allowed emerging developmental states to drive the industrial transformation process through state-owned enterprises (SOEs) and the promotion of an incipient industrial bourgeoisie; (c) the external support provided by the US government in its fight against communism, opening policy space for countries such as Japan, Korea and Taiwan to experiment with combined import substitution industrialization (ISI) and export-oriented industrialization (EOI) in different sequences (Amsden 2001; Whittaker et al. 2020);[3] (d) the role of carefully managed FDI in bringing technology transfer and capital; and (e) a relatively educated, trainable workforce, which contributed to the rise of labour-intensive manufacturing, especially when labour disciplining and repression was exercised.

---

[3] The historical political economy of late development questions the dichotomy between ISI and EOI approaches, since failures can be found in both strategies in specific countries and times, while carefully sequenced combinations seem to have resulted in the most effective and long-lasting outcomes (Amsden 2001; Oqubay 2020).

Third is the case of 'compressed development' industrializers (Whittaker et al. 2020), of which China is a leading example, involving: (a) the global rise of an organizational and technological network paradigm, which in turn facilitated the fragmentation, interconnections and complex organization of global production networks (GPNs); (b) global production fragmentation, with high-value activities located in HICs and transnational corporation HQs (R&D, design, innovation, branding, retail), and manufacturing assembly outsourced en masse to LMICs; and (c) technological change and innovation in logistics, alongside declining international trade costs, which together facilitated the dynamic of flexible specialization and trading in tasks (Page 2012), resulting in more widespread 'thin industrialization' (e.g. low-end basic assembly operations such as cut-make-trim in the apparel industry).

In all these structural transformation experiences, innovation, technological catching up, learning and emulation have been key, driving a transition from 'easy' light low-technology manufacturing to machine production and innovation-led industrial upgrading (Amsden 2001; Chang and Andreoni 2021). Successful industrializers have upgraded to higher productivity and more technologically intensive manufacturing using learning rents, often supported by developmental states, to help build production and organizational capabilities at both the individual and collective level (Chang and Andreoni 2021; Khan 2019). China is perhaps the most striking example of a rapid transition from mass labour-intensive industrialization – predicated on low labour costs, combined with a skilled workforce and expanding infrastructure – to an innovation-centred industrial model that has put the country at the frontier of new technologies such as robotics, AI, and green products like electric vehicles (EVs) and batteries (Atkinson 2024).[4]

There is a consensus that Africa is the least industrialized region in the world, and that most of its countries are still in their infancy when it comes to manufacturing capabilities. However, this consensus masks significant variation across countries and over time periods. Postcolonial industrialization experience in Africa occurred in three main phases (Chitonge and Lawrence 2020; Whitfield and Zalk 2020): first, an initial post-independence 'art of the possible', when several African governments used the state and state-created companies to pursue a broad-based industrialization agenda, mostly built on an ISI approach; second, the post-crisis liberalization and structural adjustment phase (1980–2010), when industrial policy was largely abandoned (with the notable exception of Mauritius) and trade liberalization and SAPs dominated

---

[4] See chart in Bloomberg News 'US Efforts to Contain Xi's Push for Tech Supremacy Are Faltering'. Bloomberg.com. 31 October 2024. www.bloomberg.com/graphics/2024-us-china-containment/?sref=okvcQ9hW&leadSource=uverify%20wall&embedded-checkout=true

the policy landscape, negatively affecting the limited industrial base of most countries; and third, an emerging revival on the back of some African leaders showing a willingness to emulate Asia's industrialization success, partly driven by participation in GVCs/GPNs as offshoring extends beyond Asia.

This inconsistent trajectory has led to two contrasting narratives: one that emphasizes 'premature deindustrialization' (Rodrik 2016), and another that suggests many African countries have suffered from 'premature industrialization', especially in the early post-independence phase (Robertson 2022). Although there is some evidence to support both arguments, it is mainly limited to specific country examples rather than applying continent-wide. Some countries did suffer from deindustrialization dynamics at the height of SAPs and trade liberalization in the 1980s and 1990s (Page 2012). Many countries that had started to industrialize, however, did not seem to have met the basic conditions proposed by Robertson (2022) for industrial take-off in their initial phases, namely high adult literacy rates (70 per cent or more); high energy production and consumption per capita (over 300 kWh); and lower fertility rates. Even so, some countries – notably Ethiopia and Ghana – have recently managed to speed up manufacturing growth despite failing to fulfil these criteria (Balchin et al. 2019). This conundrum also points to the debate on whether countries should follow or defy comparative advantage, and the resultant implications for whether African industrialization strategies should be bolder or more cautious (Lin and Chang 2009; Lin 2018; Chang and Hauge 2019).

Whether Africa has experienced 'premature' industrialization or deindustrialization largely depends on how one interprets these historical trajectories and 'moments' of capitalist development (Page 2012; Rodrik 2016, Lee 2017; Ggombe and Newfarmer 2018, Cramer et al. 2020; Robertson 2022). Thus, the recent 'renaissance' of industrial growth reflects patterns contingent on specific configurations of global, national and local forces, encompassing government policies and investment opportunities seized on by domestic, diaspora and foreign industrial capitalists. This 'contingent' industrialization includes both export-oriented ventures (e.g. Ethiopian, Ghanaian, Mauritian and Malgache industrial parks), and inward-looking ISI-like industrialization processes driven by domestic market dynamics, particularly linkages between construction and industrial development, as in Nigeria, Ethiopia and Angola (Itaman and Wolf 2021; Wolf 2024). These are real industrial growth episodes, despite an aggregate decline in African manufacturing sector's GDP share that has been driven by the effects of the commodity price boom and South Africa's sluggish manufacturing performance.

Overall, the main story of African manufacturing growth since 2000, when China's engagement in the continent accelerated, is one of dramatic variation.

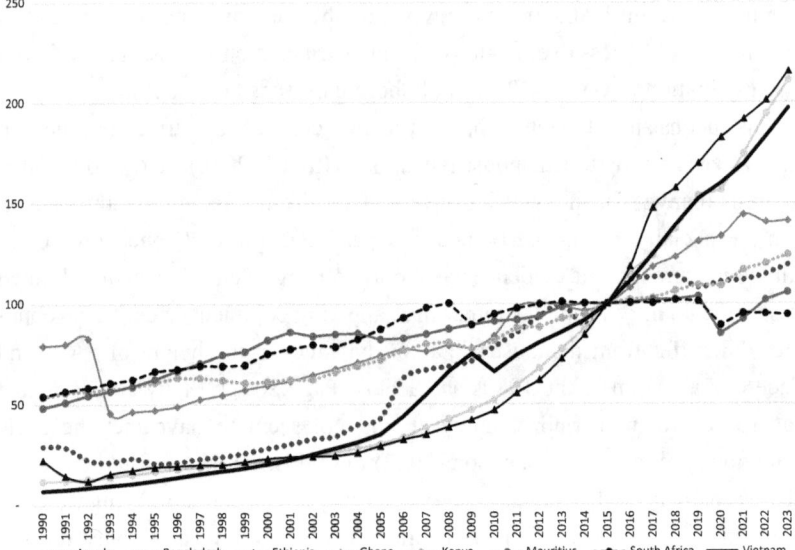

Figure 2 Manufacturing growth in selected economies (1990–2023)
Source: Own elaboration from UNIDO datasets

While some countries have – admittedly from a very low base – grown rapidly and steadily since 2000, others have stagnated or even slightly regressed. Ethiopia is the leading example of the former, and South Africa an example of the latter. The unevenness of these processes is illustrated by Figure 2, which shows how Ethiopia has since 2000 almost mimicked in relative terms the incredible industrial growth experienced by Bangladesh and Vietnam since 1990, whereas growth in South Africa – Africa's industrial powerhouse – has been remarkably sluggish over the past twenty years.

1.2 The Argument

The main thesis of this Element is that a number of opportunities for economic transformation have been generated by the rapid expansion of ties between China and many African countries, reviving the prospects for industrialization and associated job creation in *some* of these countries. The economic transformations affecting China's economic trajectory over the last two decades, especially the saturation of its low-technology labour-intensive manufacturing, and overcapacity in construction activities, underpin some of these opportunities (Lin and Xu 2019; Tang 2020). However, outcomes vary considerably across Africa, and these are still early days for recent industrialization processes.

While structural and policy obstacles mean few countries have fully exploited these opportunities yet, the relative strength and vision of national institutions, particularly the state's ability to discipline (foreign and domestic) capital, appear to be critical determinants of the success, failure or sustainability of current economic transformation experiences fuelled by Chinese official finance and state or private capital.

Furthermore, multiple barriers and contradictions stand in the way of building an industrial workforce in countries that lack industrialization experience. As such, despite industrialization offering the promise of large numbers of decent jobs, progress is likely to be slower and more uneven than expected. The kinds of investment and employment dynamics associated with Chinese-driven FDI and infrastructure development are therefore very different between, say, Angola and Ethiopia, where Chinese engagement since the early 2000s has been particularly intense. Even within Ethiopia, the fragile political settlement has put the current industrialization model's viability in doubt, regardless of China's engagement. In sum, there is enough evidence to suggest the last two decades of engagement of China in Africa have helped lay the foundations for industrialization efforts in those countries attempting to make them. However, the impact would be much greater if African elites and their governments were more committed to and embraced the idea of 'modernizing structural change', exploring with an open mind the lessons from China's structural transformation (Opalo 2024).

This Element is not just about China's engagements in Africa. It is also about Africa's legitimate right to development and structural transformation, and the realities and prospects arising from this. As such, this Element is not just about Chinese finance and firms in Africa, but also their African workers, and how China's engagements remind us of the often contradictory, complicated, and contested process of building an industrial workforce. It is not just about drivers of Chinese engagement in Africa and their contributions to industrialization, but about how African agency shapes variations in experiences, and how the interplay between politics and economic forces is key to explaining such variation. In sum, it is as much or more about African countries (e.g. Ethiopia, Angola, Nigeria) as it is about 'Global China'.

Building on the aforementioned, this Element rejects methodological nationalism, 'which has artificially sealed Chinese phenomena within China's geographical borders' (Lee 2017, 166). By contrast, fine-grained, grounded empirical and comparative research helps transcend the trap of 'grandiose generalization in terms of hegemony, empire, and neocolonialism' (Lee 2017, 161).

The Element is based on two main sources of evidence. First, it draws on the excellent fieldwork-based scholarship exploring the extent to which China's engagement in Africa promotes industrialization, and the variegated development dynamics this has brought about (Sun 2017; Brautigam et al. 2018; Oqubay and Lin 2019; Chen 2021; Calabrese and Tang 2023; Tang 2023; Zhou 2023; Mamo 2024;), along with a large set of secondary sources (data and literature).[5] Second, it employs primary comparative evidence collected by the IDCEA project (Industrial Development Construction and Employment in Africa) on employment dynamics in manufacturing and infrastructure construction, conducted over three years of fieldwork (2016–2019) in Angola and Ethiopia.[6] The latter research includes one of the largest quantitative surveys yet conducted of African workers employed by Chinese and other firms in these two sectors, garnering responses from over 1,500 workers in almost 80 firms, of which 31 were Chinese (Oya and Schaefer 2019). The project also conducted over 270 qualitative interviews with company managers, government officials, workers (several life-employment histories), international agencies, industry experts, and other key informants in different phases.

The implications of this analysis for broader debates on development in Africa are significant. At a time when post-development and new decolonial narratives abound, it is important to recentre Africa's plight in the challenges, opportunities, and contradictions of real development. This includes taking account of the legitimate aspirations held by most Africans to achieve structural change, material improvements, and socio-economic progress, while not ignoring the violence and tensions in the processes of capitalist transformations. The term 'modernization' is often used in 'Global China' discourses, and has increasingly been appropriated by African elites and intellectuals. Ordinary Africans deserve better roads, transport connectivity, access to electricity, health facilities, more and better jobs – precisely the outcomes we associate with 'development'. The quest for African 'modernity' is no longer simply a colonial project, but reflects the desires of millions of ordinary Africans and their elites (Mkandawire 2005; Opalo 2024). Opalo and Taiwo, two renowned African intellectuals, have echoed the words of the late Mkandawire (2005, 14) in issuing a call to embrace 'African modernity', arguing that, despite some imposed undesirable 'development models', 'the objective of development in the broad sense of structural change, equity and growth [is] popular and internally anchored'.

---

[5] The literature reviewed is unavoidably selective due to space constraints. High-quality primary research, thematic relevance, and variety of contexts were the main criteria to prioritize among a very large volume of available studies.

[6] See www.idcea.org for more details and resources.

2 China's Engagements in Africa Supporting Industrial Development

2.1 Framing 'Global China' Contributions to Africa's Industrialization

Having established the desirability of structural transformation through industrialization in Africa, this section offers an overview of the extent to which China has contributed to emerging industrialization efforts since the early 2000s, and the main mechanisms used.

In particular, two major mechanisms are examined in this section. First, facilitation of a substantial expansion in economic infrastructure from a very weak base, especially the kinds of infrastructure most likely to enable manufacturing development – namely, energy, transport, and industrial parks. The funding and building of such infrastructure may be regarded as central contributions, and indeed the basic foundations, of industrial development. Thus, while the relevant infrastructure does not guarantee industrial development, it does constitute a necessary precondition. Second, in the absence of an experienced, developed indigenous industrial capitalist class, the arrival of manufacturing investors in the form of FDI plays a central role. FDI-driven industrialization has been a key characteristic of 'compressed development' era (Whittaker et al. 2020). The section summarizes and evaluates evidence at continental and country level (for selected country cases) about the volume and trends of official finance, infrastructure building, and FDI, with a particular focus on what is relevant for processes of industrialization.

Variation in outcomes also depends on the scale and nature of the 'varieties of capital' entering African countries. Three key types dominate the landscape of Africa–China encounters: (a) state finance capital (policy banks like Eximbank); (b) SOEs in construction services; and (c) private manufacturing firms. Here, the 'varieties of capital' concept allows for more fluid theorization, and encourages awareness of adaptations to different political, economic and social contexts (Lee 2017). Compared to more seasoned Western firms, Chinese varieties of capital often lack overseas experience and may therefore be more vulnerable to unexpected shocks and events (Lee 2017, 160). In addition, Chinese state capital may differ from global private capital in applying the logic of 'encompassing accumulation' rather than being solely driven by shareholder value maximization. Thus, some Chinese companies may be driven by pure profit maximizing while others combine profits and market expansion, with more complex combinations potentially occurring involving profit, political patronage, and influence (diplomacy), as well as access to commodities at source.

Overall, the increasing flows of Chinese development finance, construction services, and FDI over the past two decades have taken place in the context of China's intertwined challenges of overaccumulation and overcapacity in certain productive sectors, and the governance and legitimacy of the country's development model (Hung 2008; Lee 2022; Strange 2023). These logics of accumulation and 'going out' are determined by the combined effects of 'variety of capital', sector, host country factors, and connections with other actors in China and host countries. In turn, their developmental impacts hinge on the extent of linkages with other sectors, technology transfer, spillovers to other domestic firms, generation (or saving) of foreign exchange, job creation, skill development, and the contribution to easing binding constraints on structural transformation.

Combining these perspectives, it is possible to depict a set of essential vectors that can potentially (and actually) contribute to Africa's industrialization efforts, as demonstrated by Figure 3. Two vectors dominate: first, the funding and building of key economic infrastructure conducive to industrial investment, notably energy, transport, and industrial hubs; and, second, direct investments in the manufacturing sector, typically by private firms – especially those that have GVC experience and contribute to Africa's manufacturing exports – and represented by FDI flows.

Key channels of global China's contribution to African industrialization efforts

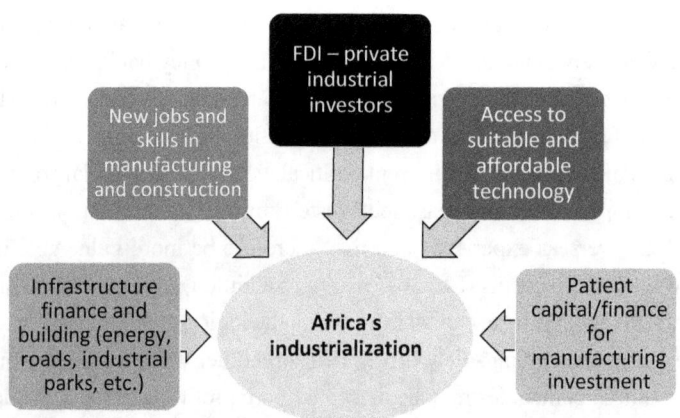

Figure 3 Key channels of China's contributions to Africa's industrialization
Source: Own elaboration

These two vectors are intimately linked to three other important mechanisms. First, contractors and manufacturing investors create new jobs for local workers in manufacturing production or construction, providing not just livelihoods to thousands of Africans, but new skillsets that are often acquired on the job and over time provide an effective basis for industrial development. The transfer of organizational capabilities (as in factory management and work) is a long-standing enabler of sustained industrialization, evidenced by the work of Amsden and Hirschman. As Amsden (2012) insists, the mass creation of jobs in viable enterprises and higher productivity sectors contributes to 'manufacturing' experience by creating an emerging industrial workforce with skills deployable across different sectors as other investment opportunities arise.

Second, manufacturing and construction investors often come with technology and capital equipment potentially suitable to the conditions of African markets. When this technology is affordable, there is potential for spillover effects onto domestically owned firms, which may contribute to industrial eco-systems clustered around specific sub-sectors, eventually inducing new activities and investments (Best 2018). The imported technology's suitability and affordability is critical in this case, with the establishment of direct linkages between foreign investors and local suppliers a necessary step in the process (Tang 2023). These are not automatic but can be incentivized by industrial policy interventions.

Third, industrial development in low-income country contexts is inherently risky – certainly more so than other activities that have tended to attract the attention of domestic capitalist classes, namely finance, trade and real estate (Goodfellow 2020). Thus, the availability of patient finance – not just for large economic infrastructure projects but for manufacturing investments, especially industrial hubs – may be crucial to unlocking profitable investments that might otherwise go unfunded, especially in contexts where capital markets perceive a high-risk business environment. Indeed, lack of access to finance is typically a major constraint for local African manufacturers and an impediment to further growth (McMillan and Zeufack 2022). As such, long-term finance on terms that are favourable to the development of industrial eco-systems is likely to contribute to more sustained industrialization, regardless of whether it is driven by FDI. When patient finance for local entrepreneurs is missing, FDI becomes one of the few realistic vehicles for industrial development and technological catching up.

The following two subsections unpack the dynamics of expansion of Chinese-funded and -built infrastructure and Chinese FDI into the manufacturing sector. For both phenomena the main implications for Africa's industrialization are teased out, given the evidence to date.

2.2 Financing and Building Infrastructure for Structural Transformation

2.2.1 The Centrality of Economic Infrastructure in Structural Change

The past two decades have seen a construction drive across Africa, coinciding with the arrival of Chinese finance for infrastructure and Chinese construction companies, broadly reflecting a global expansion of China's infrastructure industry (Goodfellow 2020; Strange 2023; Gambino and Bagwandeen 2024, 205; Dappe and Lebrand 2024). Beyond infrastructure's overall importance for economic development and legitimacy vis-à-vis society, there are three specific reasons why supporting the development of *basic economic infrastructure* is critical for industrial development in Africa and anywhere.

First, electricity matters. Any industrialization process is energy-hungry – ever since the first industrial revolution, the availability and use of cheap energy has been a foundational factor (Allen 2011; Robertson 2022). Investments in power generation capable of providing lower electricity costs and a reliable power supply to factories are necessary conditions for establishing well-run, competitively costed factories, especially when competing in global markets. In our firm surveys, a key reason given by most foreign investors for setting up apparel factories in Ethiopia was cheap, reliable electricity, facilitated by substantial investments in hydropower generation. Here, both electricity production/consumption capacity and prices matter. Ethiopia and Angola now have electricity prices of about 3.6 US cents per kWh, among the cheapest in Africa and lower than Bangladesh and Egypt (both at 9.7 US cents). However, in terms of electricity consumption per capita, both Angola and Ethiopia remain well short of other late industrializers and Robertson's thresholds of 300-500 kWh per capita. Even so, Ethiopia has seen a very significant increase over the past 10–15 years thanks to major investments in hydropower generation, which has in turn serviced a growing number of industrial parks. In Africa, only highly urbanized countries with some energy-intensive industries have reached very high levels of electricity consumption per capita (e.g. South Africa).

Second, countries aspiring to develop manufacturing through participation in GVCs need infrastructure that facilitates trade. Lower transportation and logistics costs are crucial not only for enhancing export competitiveness, but fostering more integrated domestic and regional supply chains (World Bank 2021). In an era when Africa's regional trade is promoted through the African Continental Free Trade Area (AfCFTA), regional connectivity is a must. Investments in expanding road networks, railways, ports and logistics infrastructure are fundamental to building robust industrial eco-systems, a principle that has guided industrial development both historically and today. Transport infrastructure is of course also instrumental to the expansion of home markets, which too are essential for sustained industrial transformation.

Third, East Asia's experience of industrialization underscores the importance of dedicated industrial hubs that can help realize agglomeration economies, strengthen intra- and inter-sector linkages, and reduce the costs of accessing essential infrastructure – factors critical to sustained industrial growth (Oqubay and Lin 2019; Oqubay 2022). Moreover, industrial hubs play a key role in managing migrant workforces, facilitating adaptation to rapid social and labour market changes, and helping build an industrial workforce (Oya and Schaefer 2020; Gebrechristos 2025).

The aforementioned infrastructure areas are, in fact, the three that China has placed most emphasis on in its own quest for accelerated industrialization (Brautigam 2019). Chinese engagement in Africa's infrastructure finance since 2005 has been considerable, whether through provision of patient finance for basic economic infrastructure or direct involvement in strategic infrastructure projects. This is important because, when combined, deficits in these three key infrastructure areas hinder structural transformation and future growth. The challenge, however, is that consistent investments in the three areas are needed over long periods of time. Overall, the African Development Bank (ADB) estimates that 'poor infrastructure shaves up to 2 per cent off Africa's average per capita growth rates' (ADB 2018, 73).

2.2.2 Chinese Development Finance in Africa

How has China contributed to Africa's recent infrastructure drive? One leading mechanism is dedicated infrastructure finance, mostly concentrated in the first two of the aforementioned three areas. While industrial hubs (or special economic zones, SEZs) have also received some backing, these have received lower Chinese official funding volumes and attracted a wider range of players, including private companies and provincial government agencies, as in the Eastern Industrial Zone (EIZ) of Ethiopia, one of the two largest industrial hubs in Africa (Brautigam 2019; Oqubay 2022; Chen 2024).

Figure 4 indicates the overall trend between 2000 and 2023. During the period 2011–2019, Chinese loans from policy banks – mostly going to infrastructure – hovered around the $10bn–15bn mark annually, two-thirds of which went to power and transport alone. This compares with a total annual infrastructure finance average of $77bn in 2012–2017, of which $20bn came mostly from OECD countries, making China the single largest financing source, bilateral or multilateral (Gu and Carney 2019, 154; ICA 2018). This volume of Chinese funding is also relevant to the estimated infrastructure *gap* of between $70bn

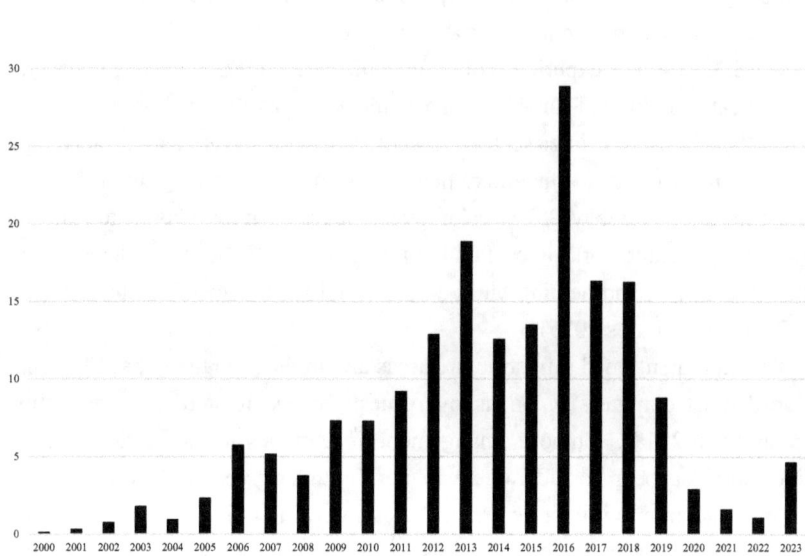

Figure 4 Chinese loans to Africa (US$ bn)
Source: Boston University Global Development Policy Center. 2024. Chinese Loans to Africa Database. Retrieved from http://bu.edu/gdp/chinese-loans-to-africa-database

and $108bn per year, as estimated in 2015 and 2018 (Dethier 2015; African Development Bank 2018). This is not a negligible proportion, considering there are multiple lenders operating in the continent, with the World Bank as the leading development finance source in most African countries.

Recent trends in Chinese development finance point to shifts in mood and modalities. Although the volume of policy bank development finance for infrastructure seemed to dry up in 2020–2022, it rebounded to some extent in 2023 (Figure 4; Engel et al. 2024), directed at several familiar suspects among borrowers (Angola, Egypt, Nigeria) and project types (power generation, transport). At the same time, it revealed some inclination towards smaller, leaner, 'greener' infrastructure projects. Meanwhile, and especially since 2015, state-owned commercial banks increased their share of financing, up to 40 per cent of total lending to Africa in the most recent estimates (Wu and Chen 2024). This diversification in credit sources reduces the risks faced by Chinese financial institutions, especially the exposure of policy banks such as Eximbank, but makes some of the new debt more commercially oriented and therefore similar to what African governments get from Western commercial creditors. The main difference in 2023 was a significant Chinese commitment towards the financial sector, notably African multilateral banks (Afreximbank, Africa Finance

Corporation) and some national banks, with a portion of this funding potentially dedicated to infrastructure. This new trend perhaps signals 'a risk mitigation strategy that avoids exposure to African countries' debt challenges' (Engel et al. 2024, 2).

The top five recipients of official loans accounted for practically 50 per cent of China's whole policy bank loan portfolio to Africa during the period 2000–2023, with Ethiopia and Angola alone accounting for a third of loans (Table 1). Although most African countries received some official finance during this period, the concentration of loans is significant. This is despite the figure for Angola skewing the results, especially given the massive refinancing package the country received in 2016, which did not bring fresh finance and included recapitalization of the leading national oil company Sonangol (Acker et al. 2020). More generally, the concentration of infrastructure finance is a driving factor behind the variation of outcomes in China's contribution to industrialization across the continent.

There are two distinct advantages to the development finance provided by Chinese state institutions, especially policy banks. First, they overwhelmingly focus on much-needed hard economic infrastructure (roads, ports, power generation) and productive sectors, which is particularly critical following decades of underinvestment in these areas (Figure 5; Brautigam 2019).[7] By contrast, the World Bank – the key development bank for Africa – currently devotes only about 30 per cent to infrastructure, including about 25 per cent for transport,

Table 1 Distribution of Chinese loans to African countries by top recipients

Rank	Country	Total Chinese loans (2000–2023) (US$ mn)	% of total
1	Angola	46,047	25%
2	Ethiopia	14,529	8%
3	Egypt	9,748	5%
4	Nigeria	9,591	5%
5	Kenya	9,589	5%

Source: Calculated from Boston University Global Development Policy Center. 2024. *Chinese Loans to Africa Database*. Retrieved from http://bu.edu/gdp/chinese-loans-to-africa-database.

---

[7] Funding for industrial activities is not a new phenomenon, as some of the old cooperation projects in the 1960s had a distinct industrial bias, for example, the Friendship Textile Factory in Tanzania established in 1968 (Brautigam 2019, 141).

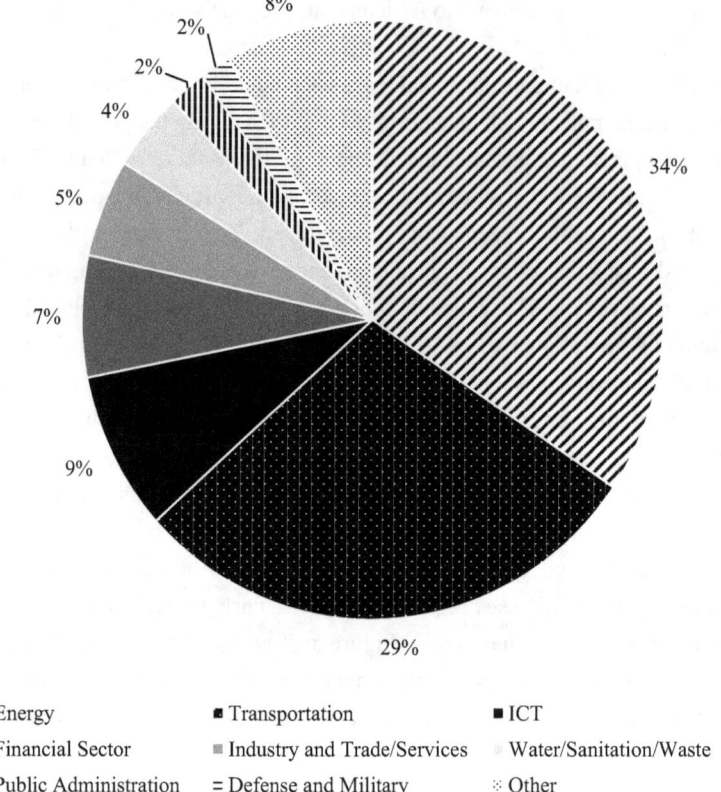

Figure 5 Distribution of Chinese loans to Africa by sector by % (2000–2023)
Source: Calculated from Boston University Global Development Policy Center. 2024. *Chinese Loans to Africa Database*. Retrieved from http://bu.edu/gdp/chinese-loans-to-africa-database.

energy and mining combined, which is well below the figures for Chinese finance.[8] In the SAPs era of the 1980s and 1990s, the share was even lower.

Given the World Bank's core remit, at least until the 1970s, has been to finance hard infrastructure, this appears paradoxical. Over the past three decades, African countries have persistently made use of World Bank funding, but deindustrialization or reverse structural change has nevertheless occurred in many of them (McMillan et al. 2014), especially in the 1980s and 1990s. Why? In answering this question, it is important to focus on the sector allocation of

---

[8] Usman (2023), find in https://carnegieendowment.org/posts/2023/04/africa-matters-to-the-world-banks-global-role-and-heres-how?lang=en.

loans and associated donor imperatives in Africa during this period. For too long, this development finance has been reoriented towards priorities aligned with the new 'consensus', whether liberalization, structural adjustment reforms or the 'good governance' agenda – in short, policy reforms. By contrast, the funding of basic economic infrastructure did not feature prominently in such imperatives. When Chinese funding started to grow to substantial levels around 2010, the economic infrastructure situation facing African LICs was abysmal. Not only were road/railroad density and relative electricity-generating capacity much lower than in other developing regions (respectively, a third and 40 per cent of South Asia's levels), but these indicators either worsened or barely improved between 1990 and 2012 (Calderon et al. 2018). This a serious indictment of the paltry efforts African governments and their main infrastructure finance backers (notably the World Bank and the European Union) made before Chinese lenders emerged.

A second advantage of Chinese development finance in Africa (and the Americas for that matter) is its inclination to act as 'patient capital', especially when policy banks are the source (Eximbank and CDB – China Development Bank). Kaplan (2021) argues that China's overseas development finance is a distinct form of patient capital involving long-term risk tolerance (hence 'patient') and absence of policy conditionality, contrary to the traditional practice of Western lenders. This is particularly the case for policy banks such as Eximbank, which follow the logic of 'building ahead of time', rather than the more narrow-minded, cost-benefit approach favoured by traditional financiers, who base their lending on shorter-term estimated rates of return, when demand for infrastructure is already latent (Lin and Wang 2017; Gu and Carney 2019). This also reflects a public investment-led approach, in contrast to the tendency of other development banks to promote private sector solutions (Gu and Carney 2019, 158). An important advantage of 'buying ahead of time' is that infrastructure is built when construction costs are lower compared to when the need becomes urgent (Lin and Wang 2017). As Hirschman (1967) argued in *Development Projects Observed*, the long-term (positive) unintended effects of large, risky infrastructure projects (principle of the 'hiding hand') are essential for learning when it comes to economic transformation processes. Such projects, however, require long-term commitments on favourable terms. This has largely been the case for Chinese finance, which often comes from institutions such as Eximbank or CDB. Although not always concessional, there has consistently been long negotiable maturity and significant debt relief, flexible debt management, and adjustments in loan conditions (Acker et al. 2020).

The rapid, large increases in finance towards long-term maturity infrastructure projects in high-risk African countries (Angola, Nigeria, Ethiopia) attests to the degree of 'patience' in Chinese development finance. Unconventional approaches to risk management have also helped, as the 'Angola model' shows, whereby Eximbank negotiated further security by linking its loan to future oil stream income that would involve a Chinese oil firm importing the fuel (Brautigam 2019; Large 2021).[9] This meant Eximbank was able to extend large credit lines with relatively limited risk, as disbursements would be linked to repayments in a China-based escrow account.

Finally, the degree of 'patience' in development finance facilitates a drive to leapfrog technology and business model changes, particularly in the case of digital technologies, where both Chinese lending institutions and major ICT firms like Huawei have established an important footprint in many African countries (Gu and Carney 2019). These higher-risk ventures can potentially accelerate structural transformation in the coming decades if such commitments are sustained.

Of course, patience is not limitless, and not all Chinese banks offer the same terms and conditions. Some are more commercially and short-term oriented, and less focused on the green infrastructures of the future (Wu 2024; Wu and Chen 2024). Recent trends suggest Chinese development finance institutions are running out of patience and since 2019 have become more risk averse, especially given evidence of debt distress and repayment difficulties among some high African borrowers (Angola, Zambia, Ethiopia), indicating that some rebalancing in Chinese loan commitments is needed (Wu and Chen 2024). Responses have ranged from debt relief or cancellation to rebalancing towards smaller, less risky projects (Acker et al. 2020; Wu 2024). The decline in funding volume since 2018 represents a worrying trend, as the need for patient capital to fill Africa's infrastructure gap is far from over. On the contrary, as more African countries seek to industrialize, infrastructure needs are only likely to grow faster. Sustaining 'patient capital' flows therefore remains a priority, even taking into consideration debt stress situations. The trade-off between potential debt distress and lack of sufficient long-term finance is real, and needs addressing through a coherent, carefully managed structural transformation plan.[10]

Overall, despite the recent decline in Chinese loans, the rapid growth in infrastructure finance and Chinese infrastructure contractors (more next) may have laid the foundations for further structural transformation in a number of

---

[9] Another example is the lending arrangement for the Bui dam in Ghana, where future cocoa and electricity revenues were linked to the loan (Brautigam 2019, 144).

[10] It is also important to note that in the past many African countries facing debt distress, or even defaulting, incurred unsustainable liabilities principally due to debts incurred in global financial markets or owed to private creditors – not exactly examples of 'patient finance' (Brautigam and Rithmire 2021).

countries. It has certainly contributed to reversing the trend of ever-growing infrastructure funding gaps in Africa. As the next subsection will document, aside from the broader role of infrastructure in structural change, the flood of new projects and contractors also creates demand for local construction material manufacturing, inducing further investments in these sectors. In this respect, the strong direct and indirect linkages between basic economic infrastructure and industrial development are well established.

2.2.3 Chinese Contractors and Infrastructure Development

The second key mechanism supporting African economic infrastructure is the direct participation of Chinese contractors in infrastructure design and building, usually through engineering, procurement and construction (EPC) projects. This is perhaps even more remarkable than the increase in loans. Figure 6 shows a surge in the gross annual revenues of Chinese companies' construction projects in Africa from less than $2bn before 2003 to a peak of over $50bn in 2015, with a slowing down thereafter. This dramatic rise closely followed patterns in Chinese official finance, though the ratio of Chinese finance to

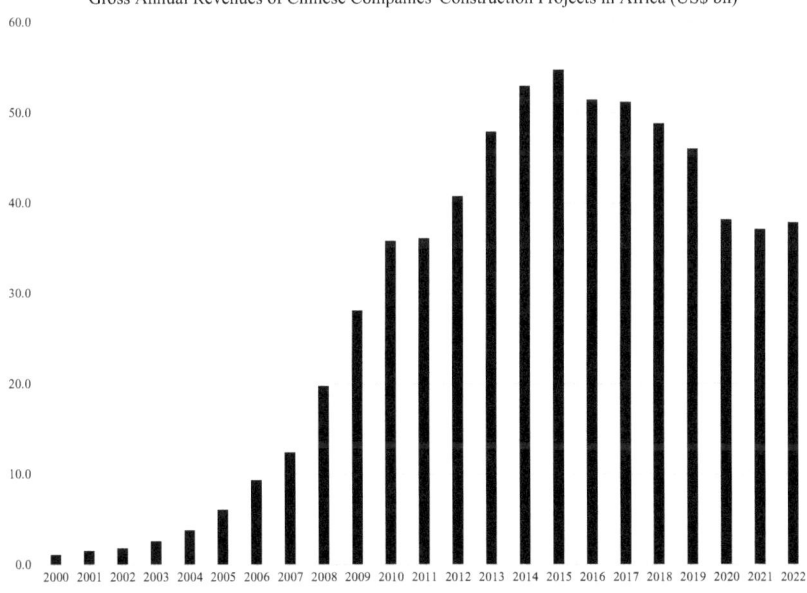

Figure 6 Gross annual revenues of Chinese companies' construction projects in Africa (US$ bn)

Source: Calculated from CARI database www.sais-cari.org/data-chinese-contracts-in-africa

contractor revenues ranges from 40 per cent in the Democratic Republic of Congo to less than 20 per cent in half the sample of African countries, suggesting a greater reliance on other sources of finance (Zhang 2021, 7). As a result of this rapid expansion, Chinese contractors accounted for over 60 per cent of Africa's construction and infrastructure market by 2019, up from only 10 per cent in 2003 (Zhang 2021). In Ethiopia, Chinese companies participated in about 60 per cent of all road works between 2000 and 2019. For both road and railway projects, most of the funding actually came from the Ethiopian government through their multiple partners (African Development Bank, World Bank and Arab development finance institutions) (Cheru and Oqubay 2019, 294). The Africa market also substantially grew in importance as a share of Chinese construction companies' gross annual revenues, from 13 per cent in 2001 to a peak of 37 per cent in 2014 (based on data from China Statistical Yearbook).

The main reason for this success is that, despite obvious finance-tying (Chinese firms being the sole eligible contractors for Chinese-funded projects), these firms are highly competitive when it comes to both technical and financial specifications (Zhao and Shen 2008; Zhang 2021), with their vast experience in China's infrastructure market compensating for lack of overseas experience (Zhou 2022). In the very segmented Angolan market, some Chinese contractors operated at lower margins to expand their market shares (Wanda et al. 2023) and not at the expense of quality, as a recent comprehensive study has demonstrated (Kenny et al. 2025).

Most Chinese contractors are SOEs, from both central and provincial levels, and operate on EPC terms. This means they often organize the subcontracting schemes in the projects they execute under the agreed arrangements with the local client (usually an African government), and can accommodate tight margins. These firms constitute a particular variety of Chinese state capital distinct from other forms of state capital engaged in mining, in the sense that 'instead of resource scarcity, the impetus for the construction sector to go global was overcapacity', driven by China's own incentive systems to promote and subsidize growth at local and macro levels (Lee 2017, 24). Thus, overcapacity in China and infrastructure deficits in African countries have made for a powerful combination.

Not all infrastructure built by Chinese contractors has directly contributed to the 'economic hardware' that industrialization requires. The logic of 'encompassing accumulation' means these players have also sought to accommodate whatever their African counterparts have requested, whether for political, ideological, electoral, or legitimacy reasons, including symbolic projects (public buildings, stadiums), real estate development linked to local elites, and transport connections of dubious value (Soares de Oliveira 2015; Taylor 2019). After all, the model does not require Chinese funders and contractors to dictate the choice of infrastructure. Despite these 'distractions' from the bottom line, the fact remains that key power and transport projects have dominated the Chinese building landscape in Africa.

Indeed, it is undeniable that both development finance and Chinese contractors have made substantial contributions to the kind of infrastructure that facilitates industrial investment. For example, Ethiopia's installed electricity generation capacity increased from 814 MW to over 4,200 MW between 2005 and 2021, while in Ghana it more than doubled to reach a capacity of 5,449 MW.[11] In Ethiopia, all this expansion was through renewables, mainly hydropower. During the same period, both countries became net exporters of electricity. Chinese lenders, contractors, and input suppliers were involved in nearly all of Ethiopia's power generation projects (Cheru and Oqubay 2019, 294).

It is hard to find an accurate time series for direct contributions to basic economic infrastructure by Chinese actors. Instead, the most relevant figures are provided by a report from China's National Development and Reform Commission (NDRC), which gives an aggregate estimate for an unspecified time period, linked to the Belt and Road Initiative. More specifically, the report estimates that, until 2022, 'Chinese companies have participated in building and upgrading more than 10,000 kilometres of railways, nearly 100,000 km of highways, nearly 1,000 bridges and 100 ports, and 66,000 km of power transmission and distribution lines in African countries. They have also helped build a backbone communications network of 150,000 km in Africa'.[12] Another source refers to more than 80 large-scale power stations, more than 130 medical facilities, and dozens of sports venues and schools.[13] These impressive results are nonetheless unevenly spread, as contractor revenues, like development finance, remain highly concentrated in a group of countries including Angola, Algeria, Nigeria, and Ethiopia, with around 40 per cent of the accumulated total in 2000–2022 (estimates calculated from data extracted from www.sais-cari.org/data-chinese-contracts-in-africa).

The establishment of industrial parks, funding for which has been much more diversified (i.e. not dependent on classic loans from policy banks), are a highlight of the linkages between infrastructure development and the building

---

[11] Most recent data extracted from https://infrastructureafrica.opendataforafrica.org/vehzayg/energy-national-level-database.
[12] Quote from official news item https://english.www.gov.cn/news/202408/30/content_WS66d11c55c6d0868f4e8ea587.html and 国家发展改革委专题新闻发布会 介绍《中国—非洲国家共建"一带一路"发展报告》有关情况-国家发展和改革委员会. This quotes the 2023 'Blue Book' report by the NDRC. Also reported in CABC (2024).
[13] China International Development Cooperation Agency, www.cidca.gov.cn/2021–10/28/c_1211423912.htm.

of industrial capabilities. Latest estimates suggest that 25 Chinese-funded parks have been built and entered operation in Africa as of 2023, attracting more than 620 enterprises with cumulative investments of $7.35bn, especially towards domestic market sub-sectors (CABC 2024, 29).

There are four main reasons why the rise of Chinese contractors may be good news for Africa's industrialization aspirations. First, their capacity to swiftly execute complex infrastructure projects at relatively low cost facilitates the expansion of critical infrastructure necessary to accelerate industrialization investments. In most cases, the contractors follow an EPC approach, whereby they are directly funded by the creditor agency, bypassing potential capacity constraints on the client side (say, the national road authority) and so speeding up project completion (Gu and Carney 2019, 157).

Second, as will be discussed in Section 3, these projects create numerous jobs for African workers, despite dubious claims that most workers are Chinese. Beneficiaries of infrastructure-related jobs are often low-skilled workers from rural origins, meaning they may have the opportunity to gain transferable skills that can be applied to factory settings, as the connections between infrastructure construction and factory work in Angola suggested.

Third, insofar as economic infrastructure contributes to the development of industrial sector export capabilities by reducing the costs associated with connectivity and logistics, infrastructure improvements may ease foreign exchange constraints. There is, however, no reliable evidence on the net effect. Here, one key example is the construction of SEZs and industrial parks, which may lead to reduced foreign exchange constraints either through manufactured export promotion or import substitution, which reduces forex leakages.

Fourth, there is growing evidence that infrastructure contractors generate an 'induced demand' effect arising from building material imports linked to large-scale infrastructure development (Wolf 2024). Angola and Ethiopia are good examples, even if the scale of these linkages differs between the two countries. The sequence is as follows. A rapid infrastructure drive necessitates large quantities of building materials, especially cement and steel. In Angola, during the early days of the post-war boom, most of these materials were imported, thereby contributing to forex leakages. The rapidly expanding market stoked the interest of local and foreign investors, who sought to invest in processing facilities capable of producing cement, steel, and their associated inputs, as well as other building materials. Thus, a manufacturing sector emerged in response to these developments. In short, the demand-inducing effect of rapid infrastructure construction led to the growth of a typically domestic market-oriented manufacturing activity, an effect anticipated by Hirschman's work and highlighted by Wanda et al. (2023) and Wolf (2024) in the case of Angola. In fact, it represents a classic example of effective ISI, supported by governmental trade protection measures. Wolf (2017 and 2024) has documented this sequence using the examples of Angola, Ghana, and Nigeria, where infrastructure construction became a 'springboard for industrialization', resulting in a variegated pool of small, medium, and large manufacturing enterprises producing high-demand building materials.

On balance, a majority of studies reviewed for this Element and our own primary research suggest that Chinese-funded and -built infrastructure projects – especially in power generation, transport (trade facilitation) and industrial parks – have contributed to more greenfield investments in manufacturing production, or at the very least created favourable conditions for these to happen in future (Darko and Xu 2024; Qobo and Le Pere 2017; Lu and Liu 2018; Alden and Lu 2019; Brautigam 2019; Megbowon et al. 2019; Li and Lu 2024) Wolf 2024). A key role in this regard is reducing risk for future investors, thereby laying the foundations for private capital to find profitable opportunities in manufacturing, and becoming effective 'brokers' for first movers so that industrial 'flying geese' can follow (Lin and Xu 2019, 279). Of course, infrastructure must be targeted to facilitate such investments, with – as will be argued in both the remainder of this section and in Section 4 – a conducive, bold industrial policy framework needed to support this on a sustained basis.

2.3 Chinese Foreign Direct Investment: Varieties of Capital in Manufacturing

2.3.1 Chinese FDI Trends in Africa

As argued in Section 1, several industrialization stories feature foreign capital as a driving force. FDI-led industrialization has also become more common in the era of 'compressed development' (Whittaker et al. 2020), with an increasing number of countries attempting to industrialize through participating in expanded GVCs/GPNs. FDI to Africa has historically been dominated by investments in the resource extractive sectors, sometimes including mineral processing, where linkages and spillovers into local firms are limited (Morrissey 2012). Much of the limited recorded manufacturing FDI from Western sources has been directed at mineral processing in countries such as South Africa or Botswana (diamonds); some basic oil processing in oil-producing countries; or large aluminium smelters, as in Mozambique since 1999. FDI to services, especially banking, construction, and ICTs, also expanded after the waves of liberalization seen across the continent in the 1990s (Morrissey 2012).[14]

---

[14] Typically, the top recipients of FDI to SSA in the 1990s were countries such as Angola, South Africa, Equatorial Guinea, and Nigeria, which hosted FDI projects directly or indirectly (through basic beneficiation) linked to resource extraction. The higher percentage of greenfield

McMillan (2017) notes the growing diversification of FDI sources into Africa, driven by Chinese investments, which has also led to sector diversification away from mining and resource extraction in general. This suggests that Chinese FDI may be different from its Western equivalents, especially in those countries where the focus is on non-resource related manufacturing.

It is important to note that official data of Chinese FDI as published by MOFCOM and UNCTAD are known to underestimate true figures, as large numbers of Chinese-owned enterprises (including greenfield investments in most cases) are not registered through MOFCOM channels, particularly for lower investment volumes, therefore especially affecting estimates of Chinese FDI into manufacturing and services (McKinsey 2017; Sun 2017; Brautigam et al. 2019; Chen 2024). The aggregate official numbers for Chinese FDI in African countries presented in Figure 7 reveal a mixed picture, characterized by a number of trends. First, the speed of growth has been remarkable, especially during the period 2010–2018, when overall trends for FDI stocks in SSA were not so rosy. Over the course of this period, the overall inward FDI stock in SSA grew by 40 per cent, compared to an almost quadrupling of Chinese FDI stock.[15] In aggregate terms (all sources of FDI included), large African recipients of Western FDI (e.g. South Africa, Angola, Nigeria) experienced stock fluctuations over a flat line, or increasing and then fast declining FDI stocks after 2015, driven by the vagaries of the oil and other mineral extraction sectors. Ethiopia bucked that trend, partly thanks to fast-growing Chinese FDI into its manufacturing and construction sector – the country's overall inward FDI stock swelled from $4.2bn in 2010 to over $38bn in 2023, with Chinese firms leading the way (Cheru and Oqubay 2019, 290). The rise of Ethiopia and other African countries as FDI recipients meant the combined share of FDI received by Angola, Nigeria, and South Africa dropped from 67 per cent in 2010 to only 30 per cent in 2023. In aggregate terms, China has jumped from not registering in statistics on FDI origin towards Africa up to fourth place, closely behind France, the USA, and the UK.[16]

Second, the percentage of Chinese FDI stock in manufacturing is far from negligible but also largely underestimated in official records. This partly reflects the fact that the distribution of Chinese FDI tends to be more diversified than

---

investments going to manufacturing in recent FDI flows (average of 15 percent in value for 2021–2023, according to UNCTAD 2024 and www.fDimarkets.com), reflects the combined effects of large industrial investments in Morocco and Egypt, mineral processing in SSA, and the rise of Chinese manufacturing FDI across various countries. Services dominate overwhelmingly in the latest three years (including construction).

[15] Data extracted from UNCTAD database, https://unctadstat.unctad.org/datacentre/dataviewer/US.FdiFlowsStock.

[16] The Netherlands is technically first, but in practice acts as a transit point for FDI of various origins due to its fiscal status: https://unctad.org/news/africa-foreign-investment-clean-energy-boosts-sustainability-momentum.

China for Africa's Industrialization? 27

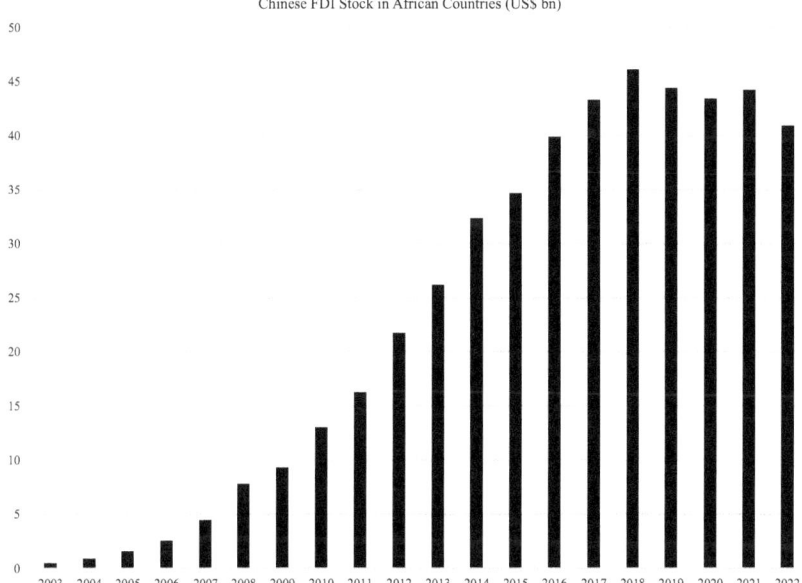

Figure 7 Chinese FDI stock in African countries (US$ bn)

Source: Own calculations from Statistical Bulletin of China's Outward Foreign Direct Investment, published by China's MOFCOM, crosschecked with database from the Center for Global Development at Boston University. Note: 'Africa' includes North Africa in this case

competing sources of FDI, which is generally more concentrated in energy-related industries (oil/gas extraction and infrastructure/supply services, and petrochemicals).[17] Although the aggregate percentage of Chinese FDI going into manufacturing (in terms of value rather than number of investment projects) has declined slightly, especially since 2019, in absolute terms it has continued to grow – from $3.5bn in 2013 to around $6bn in 2021.

Here, the reason for the percentage decline is the faster growth of FDI in construction (Figure 8), which is a logical trend given the progressive consolidation of Chinese infrastructure contractors in a larger number of countries in the years since the growth spurt began in the early 2000s. Once construction companies complete a number of projects in the same country, their next step is to establish a branch for further bidding, which is counted as FDI (Zhang 2023). In terms of *number* of greenfield projects, however, the proportion of investments directed at manufacturing is far higher – closer to a third (Shen 2015). One of the most comprehensive surveys of Chinese firms in Africa, which

---

[17] According to the author's calculations from the *World Investment Report 2024*, nearly 68 per cent of Greenfield FDI projects in the period 2021–2023 went to these industries.

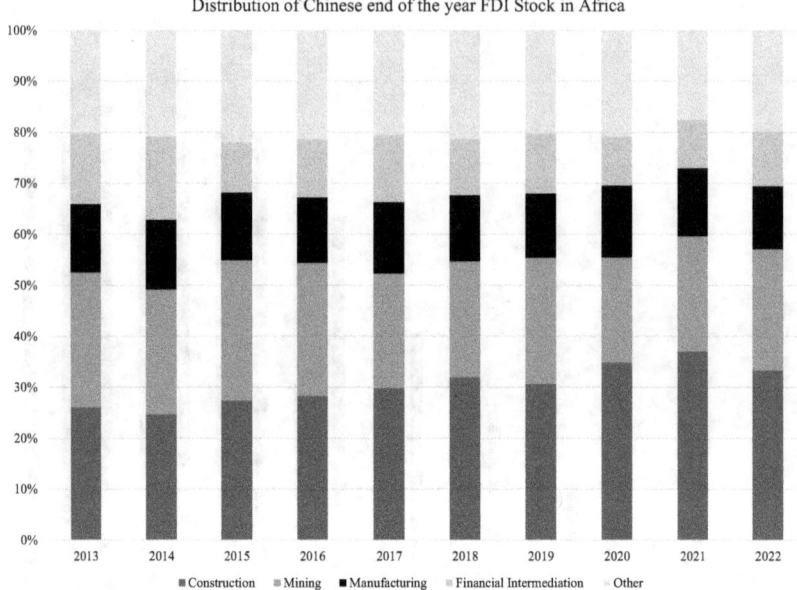

Figure 8 Distribution of Chinese FDI stock in Africa by value (%)

Source: Own calculations from Statistical Bulletin of China's Outward Foreign Direct Investment, published by China's MOFCOM as above. Note: 'Africa' includes North Africa in this case.

counted around 10,000 companies, many of which outside MOFCOM records, estimated the share of manufacturing at 31 per cent (McKinsey 2017). This divergence from the shares based on value reflect the labour-intensive, smaller-scale nature of the manufacturing sector compared to capital-intensive sectors like mining and construction, as well as the significant number of unrecorded investment flows into manufacturing.

Third, China's officially recorded FDI volumes remain too low to spur a dramatic industrial transformation in the medium run, even if a greater focus on manufacturing and construction may generate some level of industrial revival. Variation is important. While there have been visible effects on some countries (e.g. Ethiopia, Kenya, Ghana), the picture is less impressive when looking at Africa as a whole. Africa receives only a small proportion of total Chinese FDI, of which around 13–14 per cent goes to manufacturing, meaning the FDI's aggregate-level contribution is still only moderate. Many African countries have received barely any Chinese investments in manufacturing, although most of these lack the basic conditions necessary to make manufacturing investments minimally profitable at an acceptable risk. By contrast, Ethiopia during the period 2010–2020 demonstrates the potential impacts of a much larger volume and proportion of FDI going to manufacturing. According to the EIC (Ethiopian Investment Commission) data, the share of manufacturing in terms of Chinese FDI value was close to 80 per cent for the period 1998–2018, a proportion replicated in terms of number of projects (Chen 2024). This is a recent phenomenon, as even in Ethiopia – a leading recipient of Chinese industrial FDI – the flows only started surging after 2012 (Mamo 2024).

Overall, while there is a long way to go, the remarkable levels of foreign manufacturing investments directed at SSA in recent years demonstrate the potential of African countries when it comes to attracting substantial volumes of Chinese industrial investment (Sun 2017).

2.3.2 What Kind of Manufacturing Investors and Why?

Sun (2017, 44) poses the question of why manufacturing in Africa is now attracting so much investment after decades of neglect. Her answer implies that two factors are at play: one structural and one individual. While the former is the classic latecomer advantage and 'flying geese' hypothesis, the latter points to entrepreneurs' personal commitment and ingenuity (i.e. agency), particularly in situations where the risks involved would seem to discourage investment commitments. Let's unpack the realities of Chinese manufacturing FDI in SSA.

Classification: ISI vs EOI Investors

Many authors have made reference to the 'flying geese' thesis, initially developed by Akamatsu (1962) and often used to characterize FDI flows from Asia to Africa (Brautigam et al. 2018; Lin 2018; Calabrese and Tang 2023). The thesis describes the phenomenon of delocalization, with entire production lines shifting location on the basis of cost and market expansion considerations. Here, the textile and apparel industry is frequently cited (Whitfield 2022). This analogy is useful but insufficiently precise given the range of sub-sectors and drivers that Chinese varieties of capital display across different African countries, as well as the fact that the bulk of light manufacturing has remained in China despite some relocation overseas. In short, while many textile and apparel companies move to some African countries, textile and apparel exports from China remain strong. The 'flying geese' transition may therefore be a protracted process.

The effective reality of recent Chinese manufacturing FDI into Africa is that two distinct patterns can, to varying degrees, be discerned in different countries, dependent on the policy context and market opportunities. As explained in Section 1, the conventional contrast between ISI and EOI approaches and their sequencing describes the divergences in late development industrialization trajectories. This classification can also be applied to manufacturing FDI, given the different drivers and types of firms involved (for example, whereas some firms seek access to expanding African domestic and regional markets, others operate within GPNs and regard African countries as potential platforms for global exports).

The first type of manufacturing FDI – perhaps the most dominant in the present context – can be described as a manifestation of an 'ISI path', and is primarily concentrated in the building materials industries, basic household items and consumer goods. These investors are driven to tap into local market opportunities, which sometimes arise due to linkages with the construction sector boom, which may generate demand that cannot be met by imports only. Hirschman's 'induced demand' signal plays a key role here, as importers and traders may capture opportunities to invest in domestic production facilities as a means of increasing their rates of return (Hirschman 1958; Wolf 2024).

Several studies of Chinese manufacturing FDI into Africa suggest this 'path' is prevalent across a larger number of countries, particularly those with larger markets and limited manufacturing export experience, such as Nigeria and Angola (Geda et al. 2018; Xia 2021; Chen 2021; Calabrese and Tang 2023; CABC 2024; Chen 2024). Although the path encompasses a wide range of activities – from plastic recycling to plastic shoes, flip-flops and household goods – a large number of firms have focused on building materials, especially cement, bricks, ceramics and glass (World Bank 2012; Chen 2021; Wolf 2024). Another key growth industry is furniture, which has been driven by Chinese traders with small export–import businesses in relatively large markets like Nigeria, as documented by Chen (2021).The range has been widening over time, suggesting the kinds of market opportunities and entrepreneurs are actually more variegated than previously assumed. For example, there is growing evidence of new plants being established for the manufacturing of consumer electronics and appliances, including handsets, or vehicle and equipment assembly, especially trucks and agricultural machinery (Brautigam et al. 2018; Lu and Liu 2018).[18] In most of these cases these investments are not crowding out local investors and hold the potential of turning into exporters to regional and global markets if plants are scaled up.

Chinese companies see potential in capturing a share of the substantial import (domestic) market currently served by Chinese goods. As such, it is often Chinese importers who decide to invest, especially when it comes to products that are particularly heavy and so more expensive to transport (cement, ceramics), or products requiring bulky raw materials that can easily be sourced locally,

---

[18] https://www.investmentmonitor.ai/features/africas-reliance-on-china-is-only-likely-to-get-worse/?cf-view.

as in the case of furniture (lumber) and ceramics (clay) (Sun 2017; Chen 2021; CABC 2024, 22). Cement is a niche industry where Chinese manufacturers are exerting growing power across countries, from Ethiopia to Angola, and where sales by Western investors are opening new doors to Chinese capital as in Nigeria and Zambia.[19]

Other traditional sectors, such as textiles, have also been subject to this ISI path, although with some contradictory shifts. In the case of the once-booming Nigerian textile industry, 'Chinese industrialists helped create [it], then Chinese smugglers helped kill it' (Sun 2017, 41), only for a new wave of Chinese investors to revive it in order to exploit the growing size of the Nigerian domestic market and limited domestic competition (Chen 2021). This shifting dynamic is also relevant to a range of consumer goods and household items (e.g. kitchen utensils, ceramics, plastics, foam mattresses, furniture), with small-scale local industries hit by Chinese imports from the 1990s trade liberalization (Meagher 2016), only to experience a revival partly and paradoxically driven by Chinese investors hitherto involved in the import business (Attah-Ankomah 2016; Xia 2021).

One advantage many Chinese manufacturers enjoy is their vast experience in consumer good and household item standardization, which enables simple imported technology to be efficiently produced at scale. A prominent example here is the Nigeria-based manufacturer that produces flip-flops at a lower unit cost than in China, beating the price any smuggler can offer (Sun 2017, 47). Tang (2018) documents a similar dynamic in Ghana, where Chinese firms in the plastics recycling industry choose older or semi-automatic machinery for their Ghanaian operations due to the local market's lower technical demands and a perception that Ghanaian workers are low skilled. In such circumstances, an important question to ask is whether domestically oriented Chinese manufacturers generate a net positive contribution to the industrial landscape, after considering potential crowding-out. On the basis of the recorded growth of these industries during the period when the investments took place, this appears to be the case. Nevertheless, there have been mixed outcomes. In Ethiopia, for example, Chinese-owned tanneries crowded out some local suppliers in the production of raw and semi-finished skins, while the government was trying to push these new investors to export finished products. These investors were more interested in exporting raw leather materials to their parent company in China than contributing to the effort of leather processed exports to Western markets

---

[19] A very recent case is Swiss giant Holcim, which sold its cement factories to a Chinese firm in Zambia and Nigeria. www.bloomberg.com/news/articles/2024-12-01/holcim-sells-nigerian-unit-to-huaxin-cement-at-1-billion-value?utm_source=twitter&utm_content=africa&utm_medium=social&cmpid%3D=socialflow-twitter-africa&utm_campaign=socialflow-organic.

(Mamo 2024). A similar phenomenon has been documented in the textile (fabric) sector of other West African countries (Nigeria, Ghana), as well as the production of basic household utensils (Sun 2017; Tang 2018; Chen 2021). By contrast, in sub-sectors like cement, furniture, or pharmaceuticals, there is no evidence of crowding-out and fairly strong evidence of a net contribution to growth and complementarity with domestic firms (Oqubay 2015).

The second characteristic modality of Chinese manufacturing firms is the EOI path, which is much less common given the barriers to participation in GPNs. The leading example is Ethiopia, although there have been some precedents in Mauritius, Kenya, Lesotho, and, more recently, Madagascar and Ghana. Sun (2017, 9) describes many of the entrepreneurs searching for new export platforms to continue their business and operations as 'tough, gritty, unglamorous people living out adventure stories'. A survey conducted by Lin and Xu (2019) in China's light manufacturing sector to gauge key push-and-pull factors found that rising labour costs are the core determinant, exacerbated by excessive competition in China and increasingly tight regulations, especially concerning environmental standards. This is consistent with what interviewees in the IDCEA project reported, with 'push' factors playing a more prominent role than the incentives provided by host African governments, or preferential trade agreements such as the African Growth and Opportunity Act (AGOA), aimed at providing easier access to the premium US market.[20]

Despite these drivers, only a fraction of surveyed firms considered overseas relocation a viable option in the short term given that automation or relocation to lower-cost sites within China would likely be less risky (Calabrese et al. 2017). Given the limits to automation in industries like textile and apparel, however, the possibility of relocation is more likely to interest firms involved in these areas. Lin and Xu (2019) estimate that China's light manufacturing and low-tech sectors provide about 85 million jobs. Thus, even if only 10–20 per cent of such firms relocate to other parts of Asia and Africa, the prospect of 9–17 million industrial jobs is surely appealing. For countries like Ethiopia, Tanzania, Kenya, or Ghana, attracting hundreds of thousands of these jobs would be a game changer. Nevertheless, the present reality is that only a very small fraction of well-established light manufacturing Chinese firms have so far moved to Africa. It remains possible that some may expand operations overseas while maintaining higher-tech and higher-quality production in China as we observed in our research in Ethiopia (see also Lin and Xu 2019).

One of the main obstacles to accelerated growth in the export-oriented light manufacturing sector, especially apparel, is the double squeeze facing suppliers

---

[20] See also Chen (2024) on a wider set of push-and-pull factors.

in highly demanding GPNs, where global brands require continuous flexibility (capacity to quickly respond to shifting orders) and low prices (Anner 2020). This means export apparel manufacturers must keep unit labour costs down to compete with the next lower-cost competitor, and run factory operations at speed and with quality to avoid losing orders from international buyers (Whitfield 2022). This requires a workforce ready to work in high-pressure environments characterized by extremely demanding efficiency levels, where overtime is the norm, in settings equipped with adequate energy and logistics infrastructure (as we observed in our factory visits in Ethiopia). Thus, Chinese suppliers entering Ethiopia, Kenya, or Ghana are no different from other international suppliers in the sense that they bring with them global industry production and labour norms. Whether they constitute a significant flock of 'flying geese' remains to be seen, but there are indications that such relocation may continue over the coming years across a larger number of African countries, especially if continuous tariff wars and trade disruptions push more Chinese suppliers overseas.

Varieties of Chinese Capital and Accumulation Trajectories

Given these distinct patterns and varying manifestations, the range of FDI drivers, motivations, and entrepreneurial aspirations are bound to vary by sector, time, origin of firm, and experience. Here, the concept of varieties of Chinese capital is apt, even to a high degree of granularity, since logics of production, marketing, and labour regimes may differ significantly between a large GPN-linked factory exporting to the US market, a cement producer in Angola, and a flip-flop maker producing for Nigeria's domestic market. This variation is marked by the fact that Chinese-owned factories have been established – to different degrees and scales – across countries that diverge significantly in terms of size (Nigeria vs Rwanda), region (West, East and Southern Africa), and being resource-rich (Nigeria, Angola) or poor (Senegal, Rwanda, Ethiopia) (Sun 2017, 12; Lu and Liu 2018).

The diversity of capital is also rooted in the different industrial traditions within China to which such capital belongs (Chen 2024). Sun (2017, 53) proposes a 2x2 way classification based on two criteria (equating to four types): (a) whether production is labour or capital intensive (which tends to be sector specific); (b) whether production is oriented to global or domestic markets. Capital-intensive firms dominate the building materials sector but operate at quite different scales depending on what they produce, with very large cement and steel factories standing in contrast to small and medium-sized enterprises (SMEs) making bricks and ceramics. While some factories in this sector may be quite labour intensive (e.g. low-tech steel smelters), others may be capital intensive (e.g. aluminium production or cold-rolled steel, as we observed in our Angola surveys). During our research in Ethiopia and Angola, we found examples of all four classification types, with Chinese firms represented in each category, reflecting the growing heterogeneity of investors within and across sub-sectors (Chen 2024).

Each of these types is driven by different combinations of 'push' and 'pull' factors, which in turn shape their accumulation trajectories. In order of significance, the literature (Chen et al. 2018; Sun 2017; Tang 2018, Brautigam et al. 2018; Lu and Liu 2018; Xia 2021; Chen 2021; Calabrese and Tang 2023; Chen 2024) emphasizes the following 'pull' factors: (a) market access and import substitution; (b) relatively low labour costs (though there is huge variation); (c) unsaturated markets (i.e. less competition than faced in China); and, in some cases, (d) direct access to raw materials for processing (tanneries in Ethiopia). Shifting conditions in China have also 'pushed' particular varieties of capital to relocate, primarily due to rapidly rising labour costs, especially in low-technology, small-margin, labour-intensive industries (like apparel and textiles), and overcapacity and slowing growth in sectors such as building materials (Hung 2008; Lin and Xu 2019; Calabrese and Tang 2023; IDCEA firm surveys). As the aforementioned implies, these represent fairly conventional 'capitalist' accumulation strategies (i.e. escaping overcapacity; looking for lower production costs; expanding into new markets). It is worth reiterating that the vast majority of these Chinese manufacturing investors are private, essentially capitalist enterprises looking for profits and new markets.

The host context also matters in terms of which varieties of Chinese capital they attract. While Ethiopia has managed to attract some leading apparel exporters – varieties of capital deeply integrated in GPNs, and characterized by highly professional management and high efficiency levels – Angola has mostly attracted SMEs (with the exception of cement) and a particular variety of capital characterized by migrant or diaspora entrepreneurs ('translocals') (Lee 2017; Chen 2024).[21] The latter are driven by individual agency and local connections, and are very sensitive to specific (at times, very niche) investment opportunities where there is limited domestic competition and low barriers to entry. The former, by contrast, had to be persuaded to come, meaning the role of industrial policy incentives, availability of subsidized infrastructure, tax incentives, and trade preferences (e.g. AGOA) are critical.

We should not confuse the small–medium scale segment of Chinese manufacturers with informal micro-entrepreneurs, which abound in African

---

[21] In our research, we found that 'translocal firms', owned by the Chinese diaspora, were mostly registered as 'domestic' (not FDI) in industrial censuses, and had local partners as figureheads to circumvent bureaucracy. See also Rounds and Zhang (2017) on similar examples in Kenya.

production settings. In fact, McKinsey's survey of nearly 200 (mostly privately owned) manufacturing firms yielded an average annual revenue of $21 million, which exceeds the cut-off point defining SMEs in African settings (McKinsey 2017; Sun 2017, 43). Some manufacturers may therefore be small by Chinese standards, but relatively big by African standards. Most are reportedly ready to take risks and 'eat bitterness' in high-risk contexts, providing a vivid illustration of Hirschman's 'bias for hope'.

Another significant variety of Chinese capital is the 'importer/trader-new manufacturer', particularly visible in building material industries as well as in household item production. Most of these investors did not have manufacturing operations in China or other Asian countries. Instead, many arrived in African markets as wholesale traders or employees in construction projects, before becoming involved in the lucrative import business, albeit at widely diverging scales. We observed this pattern especially in Angola, while data from Nigeria, Ghana, Kenya, and Zambia suggest a similar pattern (Brautigam et al. 2018; Tang 2018; Xia 2021; Chen 2021). For example, in a sample of 22 Chinese manufacturing firms in Nigeria, over 50 per cent of investors were originally traders, and for 75 per cent access to the local market knowledge was the primary driver of their decision to invest.[22]

In sum, the varieties of Chinese manufacturing capital defy any simplistic generalizations, calling instead for a granular analysis of specific experiences, failures, and successes.

Manufacturing in Industrial Hubs

The salience of industrial hubs is an important stylized fact of Chinese manufacturing FDI in Africa. In fact, investments in setting up SEZs have also been an area of interest for another variety of private Chinese capital, focused on industrial infrastructure development and management.

Industrial hubs have become a popular phenomenon in a growing number of African countries, reflecting in part learnings from Asian experiences, particularly China's use of industrial hubs as areas for policy experimentation in the 1980s. Although the use of SEZs is not new in Africa, some African governments – Ethiopia is a clear example – have revived and embraced this industrial policy tool for its quick rewards, especially as part of an FDI-led industrial strategy (Cheru and Oqubay 2019). There are clear potential benefits to specialized clustering, especially in contexts of limited previous industrialization: shared targeted infrastructure (where this is not widely available, e.g. electricity); supply chain reproduction; shared knowhow; economies of agglomeration; and even

---

[22] Estimated from a dataset kindly shared by Yunnan Chen. See also her article (Chen 2021).

guanxi,[23] which, according to both our own field research and other studies, drove entrepreneurs to travel and invest together as 'flocks' of geese with shared industrial experience (Brautigam and Tang 2014; Tang 2018; Brautigam et al. 2018; Oya and Schaefer 2019; Chen 2024). Estimates of the impact of such Chinese-linked zones vary. The African Development Bank suggested that Chinese-funded SEZs in Ethiopia, Nigeria and Zambia had attracted more than 400 firms by 2018 (ADB 2019).[24] Oqubay (2022), by contrast, limits this estimate to 271 in seven Chinese-funded or -owned industrial hubs (China–Africa economic and trade cooperation development zones, ETCDZs) across Egypt, Nigeria, Zambia, Mauritius and Ethiopia, together responsible for an estimated total of US$3.1bn of manufacturing investments and over 40,000 jobs.

Studies suggest that the expansion of SEZs (whether Chinese funded or not) has been instrumental in attracting larger groups of Chinese manufacturing enterprises across many African countries beyond just Ethiopia – especially Nigeria, Ghana and Rwanda (Brautigam and Tang 2014; Tang 2023). Indeed, many Chinese industrial investors have set up factories in African-owned industrial hubs, with Ethiopia foremost in establishing a fast-expanding network of industrial parks (24 by 2021, according to Oqubay 2022). Despite contributing to bringing in significant manufacturing investments that might not have otherwise materialized, the outcomes and impact of these industrial hubs have been mixed. Perhaps the most positive effect has been to induce Chinese manufacturing firms' interest in African markets, while providing some African governments an opportunity to learn from the successes and failures associated with these zones (Tang 2020; Oqubay 2022).

In the case of Ethiopia, there have been spillover effects, with two investors (Huajian and George Shoes) going on to set up their own industrial hubs in other areas close to Addis Ababa (Oqubay 2022). By contrast, two of the industrial hubs that seemed most promising – Jen Fei ETCDZ in Mauritius and Lekki Free Trade Zone in Nigeria – have had disappointing outcomes due to serious implementation and management issues between the Chinese investors and local government agencies. According to Oqubay (2022), the uneven outcomes of these zones arose from a host of factors. Particularly problematic was the lack of government institutional coordination or a strategic approach in Nigeria, and the complicated ownership and management structures in Mauritius, which resulted in delays and standstills, discouraging investments. These experiences underscore the centrality of local context and government policy, as further argued in Section 4.

---

[23] 'Guanxi' (关系) is broadly understood as the system of social networks and personal interconnections which facilitate business and deals, common in the Chinese business context.

[24] Chinese provincial governments have been active in funding such hubs (Lin and Xu 2019).

A Future for Medium-High-Technology Investments?

While the evidence so far shows that labour-intensive light manufacturing and more capital-intensive building materials production are dominant among Chinese players across Africa, this is a fast-moving field. Aspirations to industrialize extend beyond the classic 'easy' light industry sectors into new green transition sectors. In an era of climate change, no serious industrial strategy can ignore the imperative of green industrialization, even if the burden of the transition should not fall on LICs (Hauge 2023).

China is fast becoming a global leader in green industries, particularly the production of green energy generation equipment and EVs (including all their components), with the country's global dominance in these emerging sectors such that its industrial capacity is set to expand overseas. This is expected to include a new wave of green manufacturing FDI in LMICs (Yu 2024; Owusu et al. 2024). Indeed, as far back as 2013, Jiangsu Tianyi Group invested in the construction of Avanti New Energy Materials Co., Ltd. in Nigeria, creating more than 4,000 jobs and putting Nigeria on the global lithium industry map (CABC 2024).[25] Promises of factories producing EVs, especially in Morocco, South Africa, and Nigeria, solar panels, or wind turbines have become part of a new narrative painting Chinese engagements as contributing to a green industrial transformation in Africa (Africa Confidential, 2024). The argument goes that the same kind of overcapacity dynamic as least partially responsible for significant investments in the heavy industries needed for building materials (cement, steel) may now apply to a new wave of investments in factories devoted to green technology goods (Chan 2024).

Similarly, some African governments (e.g. Ethiopia, Nigeria, Ghana, Senegal) have targeted other high-value-added sub-sectors with substantial local, regional and global scope. Prominent in this respect are the biotech and pharmaceutical industries, driven by a need on the part of African countries for domestic production capabilities conducive to generic drugs aimed at the local market (Mackintosh et al. 2015). Chinese manufacturers have developed competitive advantages in this field, and – should intellectual property (IP) restrictions permit – may target African markets for relocation given the significant production and export potential (CABC 2024).[26]

---

[25] The DRC, which has vast lithium resources, is being talked about as a potential site for lithium battery factories, in what could become a high-profile example of resource-based industrialization.

[26] See also the following story of an investment in Nigeria: www.bloomberg.com/news/articles/2024-09-27/china-nigeria-drugmakers-plan-to-build-plant-in-african-nation?utm_campaign=socialflow-organic&utm_source=twitter&utm_content=africa&utm_medium=social&cmpid%3D=socialflow-twitter-africa.

Spillovers and Knowledge Transfer

Transfers of knowhow and basic organizational capabilities are critical if Chinese investments are to generate spillover effects capable of contributing to the formation of viable industrial eco-systems (Best 2018; Khan 2019). In China, joint-ventures have proven essential, 'forcing' foreign investors to share technology and organizational capabilities (Nolan 2014).[27] Unfortunately, these are rarely present in African countries, which are therefore forced to rely on other mechanisms (Chen 2021). The evidence so far points to a mixed picture, but linkages and spillovers generally appear to still be limited. In other words, Chinese firms – whether domestically oriented or export led – have not yet contributed to well-articulated, 'thick' industrial eco-systems, and in some cases appear isolated in industrial parks with few spillover effects outside their boundaries, although this outcome is not limited to Chinese investors (Brautigam et al. 2018; Chen 2021; Whitfield and Staritz 2021; Kopinski and Carmody 2023; Tang 2025).

Various reasons underlie this limited impact, in particular a lack of government support to facilitate spillovers, as well as a dearth of domestic manufacturing firms ready to appropriate the knowhow and capabilities shared by foreign investors (Section 4). Of course, there are many contexts where Chinese firms rely on local suppliers, especially in some building materials industries or furniture making, but this has not led to sustained growth in associated industrial eco-systems (Chen 2021; Wolf 2024). The fact that many Chinese companies operate in sectors with relatively simple technologies, meaning less sophisticated managerial skills and training are required, may also limit key managerial skills transfer (Brautigam et al. 2018; Ellis et al. 2021). On the other hand, some studies suggest that the arrival of Chinese industrial machinery may gradually contribute to industrialization efforts through providing more affordable, suitable technology and capital equipment to emerging domestic small- and medium-scale manufacturers in labour-intensive sectors (Chen et al. 2018; Jenkins 2019; Chen 2021). In Kenya and Nigeria, for example, there is evidence that the arrival of affordable machinery has contributed to the expansion and scaling up of local small and medium manufacturers producing for domestic/regional markets (Atta-Ankomah 2016; Chen 2021).

Localization of the management workforce, especially production management, can contribute to tacit knowledge transfers in the form of experience with global sourcing customers, and understanding of standards and technology. Eventually, this can then be carried over when local senior managers become entrepreneurs in their own right, or move to manage the factory floor in domestic

---

[27] Bangladesh offers another example of this successful practice (Khan 2019).

firms (Morrissey 2012; Oya et al. 2022). In African countries with limited managerial capacities, however, foreign firms – especially those linked to GPNs – tend to assign key senior positions to expat managers, thereby reducing the scope for knowledge transfer. Evidence is mixed over whether Chinese firms are less likely than other foreign firms to localize senior management positions (Ellis et al. 2021; Oya et al. 2022; Ackah et al. 2024). Joint-ventures involving shared management between local and foreign employees are more likely to lead to organizational capability transfers in the medium to long run, but this approach is unusual in most African manufacturing sectors (Tang 2018; Chen 2021). By and large, the most effective knowledge transfer mechanism among Chinese manufacturing firms in Africa remains the informal training of workers through 'show and tell' and the upgrading of the best trained to production management positions, a phenomenon increasingly documented in the micro-level firm literature (Chen 2021; Park and Tang 2021; Gebrechristos 2025; Tang 2025).

Overall, the evidence suggests there is still a long way to go before Chinese and other sources of manufacturing FDI in African countries become effective, sustained sources of knowledge transfer and spillovers. Such processes are slow, however, and it may take 10–20 years before any progress can be properly evaluated.

2.4 Narratives of Industrial Cooperation: From Realities to Discourse

While Chinese manufacturing investments have been modest in terms of aggregate official FDI levels, they are nevertheless qualitatively significant in light of the dearth of capital and knowhow devoted to industrialization in Africa over the past four decades. This subsection briefly addresses whether official industrial cooperation discourses and narratives have caught up with the realities of Africa–China engagements. Has a bolder public discourse been articulated in favour of industrial cooperation on the back of actions on the ground? If so, what narratives have been forged?

The 'Global China' framework includes both a 'soft power' element, which is central to the bundle of power mechanisms (economic statecraft, patron–clientelism, symbolic domination), and a policy-strategy element, which features official discourses and documents outlining the key strategic directions guiding China's economic and political relations with African countries (Lee 2022). Cutting across the boundaries between policy and power, official narratives of 'win–win' and 'shared prosperity' – common throughout the period of enhanced relations – have permeated multiple encounters, official documents and public speeches, defining the evolution of these relations and the benefits for the African continent.

This evolution has manifested in two main ways over the past twenty years or so; roughly since the Forum on China–Africa Cooperation (FOCAC) summits began and the 'Go Out' policy was articulated in the early 2000s. First, the 'packaging' of previous engagements by Chinese state and private capital – focused on power and transport infrastructure, building of industrial parks, and manufacturing FDI – has afforded Chinese actors opportunities to highlight on-the-ground facts supportive of an 'industrial cooperation' reality. It has been relatively easy to frame these multiple engagements, often reflective of diverse bureaucratic, corporate, ministerial and private interests (Lee 2022), as coming together to form a comprehensive approach in support of Africa's industrialization (or 'modernization'), rather than a series of isolated projects and white elephants.

One example is the showcasing of 'industrial cooperation' experiences related to the design, building, and management of industrial hubs, considered particularly conducive to accelerated catching up (Wang and Zhang 2024; Zhou 2023). This has been further strengthened by Chinese provincial-level initiatives, in particular the Hunan Cooperation Framework (CAETE), which, alongside Guangdong, Zhejiang, and Jiangsu (Lin and Xu 2019; Tang 2023; CABC 2024), directly tackles industrial cooperation in the form of state–business interactions, business-to-business encounters, and bringing entrepreneurs and policymakers together to explore 'mutual benefit' projects around specialized clusters.[28] A key turning point in the evolution of a more explicit pro-industrialization narrative was FOCAC 2015 in Johannesburg, when structural transformation and industrial cooperation were laid out as a priority in 'shared prosperity'. Tangible outcomes of this new drive include the $10bn establishment of the China–Africa Industrial Capacity Cooperation Investment Fund and proactive lobbying of the G20 to commit to promoting Africa's industrialization (Large 2021, 90).[29]

Second, discourse strategies and on-the-ground facts have been used by China to promote development models/narratives that offer an alternative to the prevailing post–Washington Consensus. Although the Chinese authorities

---

[28] A concrete outcome of such cooperation platforms is the Adama Industrial Park, co-developed by the Ethiopian Industrial Parks Development Corporation (IPDC) and Changsha Economic and Technical Development Group Corporation, with mixed funding from private and government sources (Brautigam 2019; Oqubay 2022).

[29] FOCAC 2024 saw renewed commitments to support Africa's green structural transformation through funding for green energy infrastructure, as well as the promotion of (private) investments in manufacturing capacity for 'green' sub-sectors, notably EVs and solar panels (DR 2024).

initially avoided presenting China as a 'model' for African countries, based on the assumption that China's experience is unique, a narrative has since emerged suggesting African countries could draw valid lessons from China's industrialization and 'modernization' strategy while seeking their own path (Tang 2020). This is consistent both with China's principle of non-interference in African countries' internal affairs and with the idea that China has a 'comparative advantage' in financing and building economic infrastructure necessary for industrialization and trade facilitation. An emphasis on the role played by the state is also a feature of public pronouncements and agreements in China and many African countries, as governments remain the chief partners in these engagements. In this case, the narrative is that China understands the needs of developing countries better than Western partners, and so prefers to deliver concrete results rather than give lectures on the need for policy and institutional reforms. This official narrative does not hold, however, unless facts on the ground support it. Hence, China's apparent urge to complete highly visible projects with direct connections to Africa's industrial aspirations, such as ports, railways, dams, or industrial zones.

The aforementioned two manifestations of discourse and power contribute to an increasingly compelling narrative of China's role in Africa's industrial development, one that not only resonates with African aspirations for economic transformation but also offers a distinct alternative to traditional development paradigms (Soulé et al. 2024).[30]

To an extent, the discourse on industrial cooperation and the emerging narrative around supporting Africa to modernize on its own terms reflects China's tendency to promote a 'do-as-I-do' paradigm, whereby partners are supposed to follow China's example rather than the normative and somewhat ahistorical lines 'enshrined in the Western-led liberal international order' (Garlick and Qin 2024). While doing so does not necessitate African countries following a 'China development model', it does imply two important things: first, an appreciation that China's partner countries have a right to develop and industrialize using any means at their disposal, unconstrained by the normative constraints imposed by other partners (i.e. the 'right to development');[31] and second, China's successful industrialization experience holds useful lessons for other LMICs with similar aims, not least the need for policy experimentation and policy learning to 'feel the river by touching the stones'. The conclusion to

---

[30] https://afripoli.org/exploring-the-role-of-narratives-in-china-africa-relations.
[31] Xi Jinping has publicly asserted (at FOCAC 2024 and forums such as the G20 in Rio) the right of 'developing countries' (that term) to develop and modernize without interference or sanctioning moves, mostly from Western powers. This is now seen as a 'red line' www.mfa.gov.cn/eng/xw/zyxw/202411/t20241117_11527672.html.

be drawn from this is that although it is important to acknowledge that no universally valid blueprint exists, African governments should be allowed to try different strategies to achieve industrialization, many of which have already been successfully tested in a Chinese context. Section 4 offers a more detailed analysis of these policy options and challenges, and why they do not always necessarily work.

3 Chinese Firms, Economic Transformation, and Labour Dynamics: Building an Industrial Workforce in Africa

3.1 The Centrality of Labour in Industrialization

There is no industry without an industrial labour force. With this in mind, Section 3 focuses on the labour dynamics present in Africa–China encounters. More specifically, it examines how different varieties of Chinese capital encounter African workers, and whether industrialization-related engagements differ from other enterprises or sectors. The following subsection starts by asking if these engagements bring with them new job opportunities, or whether Chinese firms bring their own workers. This is followed by consideration of the nature of the jobs created and the associated labour regimes, including the extent to which labour relations in factories and construction sites are characteristic of broader industrial labour regimes, or whether they display any 'Chinese characteristics'. Empirically, the section analyses the importance of the organizational capabilities and skills development brought by Chinese industrial investors, their adaptation to different sub-sectors – some export oriented, some trying to exploit African markets – and how these lead to new types of labour regimes (Sun 2017; Chen 2024).

3.2 Job Creation and Employment Challenges in African Economies

There have been heated debates about the employment implications of China's engagement in Africa, with contribution via jobs a key aspect in judging the degree of China's contribution to SSA's industrialization (i.e. employment effects in terms of quantity, quality and sector focus). By 2050, approximately 25 per cent of the world's population will be in Africa. According to International Labour Organization (ILO) estimates, 579 million jobs will be needed in Africa by 2030, an increase of over 300 million compared to 2018 (ILO 2019).[32] More jobs in industry or sectors where the acquired skills are

---

[32] McKinsey (2023). Manufacturing Africa's Future: Jobs, Growth, and Sustainability. www.mckinsey.com/industries/public-sector/our-insights/the-path-to-greater-productivity-and-prosperity-in-africa.

transferable and relevant to structural transformation can improve the conditions for future industrialization. Of particular relevance in this regard is the construction sector, with our work life histories in Angola indicating that many current manufacturing workers had prior experience as construction labourers.

A foundational manufacturing experience is a necessary precondition for accelerated structural change. Once an industrial workforce has begun to form, the prospects improve for a further expansion in industrial or related employment. China is indeed a good example of this. Industrial working-class formation preceded the period of post-1978 opening to global markets, with a sizeable industrial workforce on the back of decades of heavy and rural industrialization, albeit concentrated in SOEs and sectors oriented towards the domestic market (Lee 1999; Frazier 2002; Lüthje et al. 2013). By the 1980s, a large disciplined industrial workforce was well established. The same cannot be said about most African countries, although there are some exceptions where industrial development contributed to a significant industrial workforce (e.g. South Africa or Mauritius) (Chitonge and Lawrence 2020).

Determining whether Chinese firms have generated much employment through their engagements in the manufacturing and construction sectors requires reliable statistics on employment by employer origin, as well as accurate estimates of workforce localization. This is not generally possible with African labour statistics, with claims about employment in Chinese firms often hard to verify and derived from anecdotal evidence. Here, we have attempted to circumvent the lack of systematic official data by combining evidence sources and proposing a job creation range in absolute terms (which is what matters for the growth of an industrial workforce). Thus, by triangulating three different sources of FDI data from MOFCOM (Chinese outward FDI on a global scale; *registered* Chinese firms overseas per sector; share of sectors in total Chinese outward FDI in Africa)[33] and average numbers of employees per firm from independent firm surveys (our IDCEA survey, McKinsey 2017, and other surveys of Chinese industrial companies),[34] we estimate a range between a very conservative minimum of 185,000 and a maximum of 2 million manufacturing jobs in Chinese firms across SSA in the period 2013–2022. The real number is likely to lie between these two extremes, with a more plausible estimate on the lower half of the range (although it almost

---

[33] It is a lower-end estimate of firms because MOFCOM databases miss out many Chinese firms not directly registered with MOFCOM, especially the 'translocal' firms mentioned in the previous section (McKinsey 2017; Chen 2021).

[34] Such as data facilitated by Yunnan Chen for a survey of 22 Chinese-owned factories manufacturing plastics, cardboard, and other building materials in Nigeria. From this and our own surveys we estimate a reasonable average of 700 workers per firm, considering different subsectors.

certainly exceeds 185,000 by a considerable degree). In the context of employment needs across Africa, these numbers may appear unexceptional, but given that most Chinese industrial firms only have a relatively recent footprint on the continent, the additional employment contribution should not be dismissed as negligible, especially after decades of neglect.

Given the larger number of construction firms and higher level of employment per firm, job creation within the construction sector will have been much greater in absolute terms than in manufacturing for the equivalent period, even allowing for lower workforce localization rates in the former sector. In our study of Angola, we found that Chinese firms had contributed to a large share of the increase in construction jobs between 2013 and 2018, ranging from 10,000 to almost 35,000 new jobs in any given year, accounting for over 65 per cent of total new public infrastructure construction jobs for 4 of the period's 6 years (Oya and Wanda 2019). Indeed, during the post-2015 oil price crisis, Chinese contractors were the main source of new infrastructure-related construction jobs.

These numbers, coupled with a systematic decline in the number of Chinese workers employed by Chinese firms across Africa,[35] suggest workforce localization levels are not as low as suggested by some popular reporting. There is some truth to the assertion that Chinese firms in Africa lean towards employing Chinese workers, even in non-managerial positions, and especially in the construction sector. Even so, this is perfectly compatible with creating large numbers of jobs for African workers.

Overall, desk reviews, alongside own survey findings in Angola and Ethiopia, point to the following findings on workforce localization involving Chinese firms. First, localization rates (the proportion of the local workforce constituted by African employees in the total workforce employed by Chinese firms in African countries) are much higher than normally assumed: the figure of 85 per cent of local employees being African yielded by analysis of nearly sixty datasets, studies, and cases across the whole continent (Sautman and Yan 2015; Oya and Schaefer 2019) is consistent with the finding of one of the largest surveys of Chinese firms in Africa, which estimates an average rate of 89 per cent, rising to nearly 95 per cent in manufacturing (McKinsey 2017, 41). There is plenty of variation underlying these figures, however, with some countries (Angola, Equatorial Guinea) experiencing much lower rates than others (Ethiopia, Ghana).[36] In our surveys of road contractors and

---

[35] From a reported peak of over 250,000 Chinese workers across Africa (including North Africa) to about 90,000 in 2022 www.sais-cari.org/data-chinese-workers-in-africa.

[36] Angola is one of the few African countries to legally impose a minimum local labour content of 70 per cent, although this is not really enforced according to our interviewees. Nevertheless, the

manufacturing plants, localization rates were on average 74 per cent in Angola (78 per cent in manufacturing), significantly lower than the average of nearly 95 per cent in Ethiopia (Oya and Schaefer 2019). More significantly, and contrary to popular wisdom, there were no Chinese workers employed in low-skilled jobs in either country.

Second, localization rates have systematically increased across sectors and countries, especially since 2010. This is reflective of the fact that, as admitted by virtually all Chinese firm managers we interviewed, there are higher costs associated with bringing over Chinese workers. The main reason given for relying on Chinese workers for some higher-skill tasks is the pressure contractors initially faced regarding expected completion times, coupled – in the case of road projects in Angola – with a lack of available time to train large numbers of local workers. As the firms settled into the new country and stabilized a local workforce with upgraded skills, the need for Chinese workers fell over time. While some studies (Corkin 2012; Tang 2016) have mentioned language and work culture barriers, our research suggests these are temporary obstacles arising from most Chinese firms being relatively new to African settings.

One area where most foreign firms – not only Chinese – have failed to demonstrate sufficient localization efforts concerns managerial workers (Ellis et al. 2021). Although interviewees cited a scarcity of globally competitive managerial candidates (in the case of apparel exporters in Ethiopia) or a lack of experience with Chinese construction standards as reasons for this, a lack of trust in local management and reluctance to localize positions close to senior financial and production management decisions also represent important barriers (Oya et al. 2022).

3.3 Chinese Firms, Varieties of Capital and Labour Outcomes: Race to the Bottom or Upgrading?

As the aforementioned shows, Chinese firms have indeed created substantial numbers of industrial and construction jobs across Africa. This in turn prompts questions concerning the nature and quality of these jobs. This subsection therefore provides an overview of the kinds of jobs Chinese investors bring, and the variations seen across sectors and firms. New manufacturing and construction jobs are arguably a manifestation of structural change in the labour market. Many of the workers surveyed as part of our research in Angola and Ethiopia were in their first non-agricultural job. This particularly applied to young women in Ethiopia's apparel industry, but was also evident among young

---

average estimate exceeds this minimum requirement, with some variation (rates could be as low as 50 per cent in some projects, suggesting policy enforcement was not the main driver).

Angolan men migrating to Luanda from the Central and Southern regions. The conditions attached to these new jobs – which tend to be more stable, paid monthly, and involve large groups of workers – differ from those typically found in agriculture and petty informal service work. They also come with different kinds of discipline and labour control mechanisms. Thus, factory and construction work represents a substantial jump in the employment histories of newly arrived workers from rural areas. That does not mean all such jobs are similar or offer comparable conditions. There is considerable variation in labour regimes, even among Chinese firms, as elaborated on next.

Do Chinese firms 'export' their labour practices, operating labour regimes that are fundamentally more exploitative than local or other foreign comparators? The idea of China 'exporting' its labour practices has proven quite popular in, especially, studies of construction work (Gambino and Bagwandeen 2024), as well as other studies concerned with working conditions in Chinese-run workplaces in Africa (Baah and Jauch 2009; Gadzala 2010; HRW 2011). A fundamental flaw in such questions is the implied notion that there is some kind of Chinese 'exceptionalism' in labour practices – a false premise that can be undermined both conceptually and empirically.

Conceptually, it rests on the notion of a particular kind of labour process linked to a firm's national origin. While the literature on 'varieties of capitalism' acknowledges that some institutional traits and social organization modes may bear national characteristics, the reality is that labour processes are fundamentally determined by capitalist labour relations – in other words, a combination of the nature of the production process; the bargaining mechanisms in place; the relative structural power of workers and employers; and the prevailing technology used (Burawoy 1985; Oya and Schaefer 2023). Empirically, an abundance of literature and evidence has documented the variety of labour regimes found in China's economy, and how these have shifted over time, particularly in light of the fast-rising wages seen since the early 2000s (Lüthje et al. 2013; Qi and Pringle 2019).[37] Careful comparative research has exposed the fallacy of 'Chinese exceptionalism' in labour relations (Chan 2015; Lerche et al. 2017). Put another way, the idea of 'exporting labour practices' is inconsistent with the variegated reality of labour regimes in China itself and similarities with sector practices elsewhere.

What, then, characterizes labour regimes in Chinese-run workplaces across Africa? Empirically, the claim that poor or 'worse' working conditions prevail in Africa-based Chinese firms has been challenged by a growing body of

---

[37] See also Frazier (2002) on long-run labour management trajectories in China's industries through different policy and production regimes, which involve an interesting mix of continuities and discontinuities, especially in the post-revolutionary decades.

evidence, which essentially shows mixed results regarding wages and non-wage conditions – all very context-specific and reflecting 'variegated labour regimes' across different kinds of Chinese firms (Akorsu and Cooke 2011; Bashir 2015, 8; Giese and Thiel 2015; Tang 2016; Lee 2017; Fei 2020b; Chu and Fafchamps 2022, 4). Our IDCEA research tackled this question by adopting a rigorous comparative analysis of job quality and characteristics in Chinese-owned workplaces, with a multi-scalar framework encompassing three levels of analysis – firm, sector, country (Oya and Schaefer 2019 and 2023).

Sector matters. Construction jobs are project-oriented, not stable and potentially more hazardous, with workers equipped with a diversity of relevant skills and greater experience able to demand a wage premium. As such, there may be significant wage variation within the same firm. Manufacturing jobs, by contrast, tend to be more stable and standardized, although with some key differences between low- and semi-skilled labour. In general, there is less variation in wages and working conditions within the same firm, and sometimes across firms within a similar cluster. However, whereas Angolan building materials firms have tended to use experienced male workers with a long tenure history in the sector, Chinese-owned firms have been compelled to rely on rural migrant workers with no factory experience. Meanwhile, Ethiopia's textile and apparel sector was dominated by a young female workforce, typically in their first industrial job, employed by mostly foreign-owned (including Chinese) firms that export to demanding global markets. The significant variation in labour outcomes between sectors and firms (wages, working hours, productivity targets, rhythm, benefits, job security, union presence) should therefore come as little surprise.

The evidence we collected, which mostly derives from our own fieldwork in Ethiopia and Angola (both survey evidence and qualitative interviews), can be summarized as follows (Oya and Shaefer 2023). First, systematic wage comparisons suggest that for the most part factors other than a firm's origin account for any variations found, with the Chinese origin of firms bearing no statistically significant correlation with wages. Differences in wages and working conditions are reflective of a workforce's marked segmentation across sub-sectors and firm types, and generally relate to local contextual circumstances. In Ethiopia, wage differences were primarily driven by individual worker characteristics; a task's required skill level; specific location effects; employment sector; and whether employers in the apparel sector were newly established foreign firms located in industrial parks (lower wages). For example, we found wages in Ethiopia's construction sector were substantially higher than those paid in the light manufacturing sector, partly due to the skills premium demanded by many of the relevant jobs. Overall, there are greater wage variations between different Chinese firms operating in these two sectors than there are between firms of different nationalities.

GPN-linked jobs in the apparel industry face somewhat tougher conditions and slightly lower wages compared to domestic firms not exposed to global competitive pressures. Here, the concentration of apparel exporters in Ethiopia's newly established industrial parks, coupled with misguided guidance on acceptable wage levels in some of them, resulted in lower average wages among firms located in such parks. In some industrial parks, our research revealed a striking convergence of relatively low starting wages among companies, indicating quasi-cartel wage-setting conditions. In fact, there are striking similarities between the labour regime prevalent across export apparel factories in Ethiopia's industrial parks and those found in many Asian countries. This reflects the transnational nature of these regimes and how host country policy priorities influence the ways in which they adapt to local contexts at the margins (Chang 2022). The Ethiopian government initially insisted on attracting 'high-quality' suppliers and avoiding 'sweatshop' conditions, hence its control over industrial park development and demands regarding basic standards of health and safety, coupled with a rejection of subcontracting schemes that could circumvent these conditions. Once most of the new investors had arrived at the government-owned industrial parks in 2015–2017, however, no minimum benchmark wages were proposed, meaning a 'low-wage' regime was inevitable from the start. Indeed, the absence of a national or sector minimum wage in Ethiopia has also contributed to this pattern, leading to a key player in the global apparel industry, Inditex, refusing to take orders from Ethiopia-based suppliers in 2017 on the basis that doing so would be contrary to its Global Framework Agreement.[38]

Second, there are some important differences cutting across company nationalities, even within the same sector. In Ethiopia, we found some unexpected variation among industrial parks and Chinese firms within the same sector, caused by higher wages in a cluster of Chinese firms located in the EIZ, the first such zone in Ethiopia. This variation arose in part due to differences in management ethos, the length of the firm's experience in Ethiopia (greater for Chinese firms in EIZ), patterns of employer paternalism, addressing the challenge of 'poaching' of workers among firms within the EIZ (leading to more wage competition among firms), and different labour control mechanisms – all quite firm- and location-specific. In a recent evaluation of a large ILO programme in Ethiopia's apparel industry (Oya and Schaefer 2024) – six years after

---

[38] See CCOO (2016) regarding this Global Framework Agreement and Inditex's visit to Ethiopia. The lack of minimum wage as a red line for Inditex was noted by a leading union representative interviewed for IDCEA project and who participated in the GFA audit in Ethiopia.

we conducted our IDCEA surveys – we found that wages were actually higher in large export firms based in industrial parks than local firms outside IPs once we controlled for individual worker characteristics (experienced male workers were more prevalent in the workforces of local firms compared to foreign-owned firms), suggesting a more rapid upward wage adjustment than in comparator firms.

Third, other working conditions vary a lot, primarily between sub-sectors – with practices often sector specific – but also between countries, that is, Angola and Ethiopia. For example, while our research revealed clear incidences of dormitory labour regimes in Chinese-owned firms in Angola (both construction and manufacturing), this was not the case in Ethiopia, a difference that sometimes applied despite the same Chinese SOE operating in both countries. This situation owed much to domestic conditions, specifically the fact that: (a) Chinese firms in Angola faced bigger constraints in mobilizing, retaining and disciplining labour than in Ethiopia, hence their decision to mobilize organized migrant workforces and house them; and (b) the Ethiopian government took a strong stance against company dormitories, especially in industrial parks, regardless of the fact that lack of adequate, affordable housing represented a major challenge for internal migrant workers employed in factories (both those owned by Chinese investors and others). In fact, in Angola the presence of *recent* internal migrants in Chinese firms stood at around 70 per cent in both construction and manufacturing samples, compared to only 29 per cent for construction employees in Angolan companies, and around 15–20 per cent for factory workers in both Angolan and other foreign firms (Oya and Wanda 2019). Of course, Chinese firms had arrived more recently than other firms in Angola. Moreover, in contrast to the construction sector in Ethiopia, where the authorities had pushed strongly for Chinese firms to hire locally in road projects, contractors in Angola were free to 'travel' with their own workforces and house them temporarily.[39]

The Chinese and other foreign firms investing in these countries do not operate in a labour market vacuum. In most African countries, the labour market context is *not* a Fordist ideal of standard employment, consisting of stable jobs, decent real wages, and some basic welfare provision. Non-standard employment, especially informal labour relations, has tended to dominate in most

---

[39] As Lee (2017, 156) notes, labour regimes operated by Chinese SOEs and global private capital display similarities 'rooted in international and industrywide tendencies', especially in construction, whereas in mining, Chinese state capital accumulation logic holds the potential to accommodate Zambian state preferences and depart from 'neoliberal' practices, with Chinese state capital refraining from retrenching labour at times of crisis/low copper prices. See also Fei (2020a) on preferences for 'compound' labour regimes in construction.

LMICs, with India a prominent example (Meagher 2016; Lerche et al. 2017). African labour markets are particularly informalized, liberalized, and exploitative, especially after decades of neoliberal interventions, and despite dated narratives about 'labour aristocracies' in formal sector pockets of certain countries (Meagher 2016). In such contexts, the provision of more stable, monthly paid manufacturing jobs with embedded training could be considered a form of labour upgrading compared to the average informal job.

Of course, as Lee (2017, 29) argues in the case of Zambia, all foreign – not just Chinese – investors can take advantage of a labour law regime already liberalized following decades of advice from international financial institutions and donors prior to their arrival, 'bringing, for example, a global industrial trend of subcontracting and job informalization'. Labour legislation and its enforcement tend to be relatively weak, hence the importance of collective worker mobilization, whether organized through unions or not. In Ethiopia, strikes became common during a turbulent period of labour relations (2016–2019), with unions seizing the opportunity for a resurgence (Oya and Schaefer 2021; Admasie 2022). Now, just six years after unions were discouraged or de facto banned from some industrial parks, most firms based in industrial parks have a union presence and established grievance and dispute-resolution mechanisms (Oya and Schaefer 2024; Gebrechristos 2025). During our research, these forms of labour conflict, while uneven across countries and locations, appeared to be fairly common, especially among foreign-owned firms. Chinese firms specifically did not seem affected by greater labour conflict: in Angola, they were actually less affected than comparable firms; while in Ethiopia, all firms, regardless of origin, faced some form of strike action (Oya and Schaefer 2019, 60).

Skill development and upgrading is often considered to be as important as wages and working conditions, especially in contexts where factory or infrastructure-building skills are scarce. Given the projected number of estimated jobs in the previous section, the scope for skills development is significant. According to a recent study, most Chinese firms in Ethiopia, Angola, Nigeria, and Ghana rely mainly on 'on-the-job' training for their African employees (Park and Tang 2021; Ackah et al. 2024). This is consistent with our own research in Ethiopia and Angola. Although some form of induction was common to all firms, most of the learning happened once workers started the job and was typically provided by Chinese supervisors or sometimes through 'shadowing' experienced local workers. Such practices were especially common in factories and generally well organized in the apparel export industry. Virtually all new production workers in the apparel industry, regardless of a firm's origin, were exposed to a basic induction, followed by continuous on-the-job training for specific tasks, as well as more generic 'soft skills'. In some (especially foreign-owned) factories in Ethiopia, the 'continuous improvement' approach using Kaizen methods has become standard. Some Chinese firms also opted for extended training visits to their benchmarking factories in China and Southeast Asia, particularly for local Ethiopian managers and production line supervisors. One cannot overstate the importance of this kind of practical, ongoing training in manufacturing, which constitutes a basic ingredient in the transfer of organizational capabilities conducive to the gradual building of industrial eco-systems (Best 2018; Khan 2019). Despite complaining about low pay and lack of career advancement, a worker with experience in at least three different factories in Ethiopian industrial parks admitted that his main reason for staying in the job was the continuous acquisition of a wide range of skills, both soft and hard, social and technical. As such, he regarded the factory 'as a school for continuous learning'.[40] This encapsulates the core idea of 'on-the-job learning' and industrial capabilities as an organic process, with learning-by-doing and emulation becoming over time the dominant driver of catching up.

While the skills upgrading of production workers is widespread and a key source of knowledge transfer, there remains a serious gap when it comes to incorporating more local managerial workers into key positions. Facilitating learning at this level is crucial, especially in production management and marketing/sales. Our study and many others highlight the implications of this gap in terms of more limited spillovers on domestic industry (Tang 2018; Ellis et al. 2021; Oya et al 2022; Ackah et al. 2024). Although this is a common problem across foreign-owned firms, particularly those involved in export-oriented manufacturing, Chinese firms – family businesses especially – appear particularly reluctant to employ local managers in more senior positions (Oya et al. 2022). Most studies on knowledge transfers in manufacturing FDI conclude that this poses a critical barrier to sustained industrial development in most African countries, and should therefore be treated as a policy priority.

3.4 The Contemporary African Realities of Building an Industrial Workforce: Resistance and Contestation

Despite some early studies reporting a high incidence of labour conflict and fractious labour relations in Chinese-owned workplaces in Africa (Baah and Jauch 2009; Gadzala 2010), the evidence for such workplaces being more conflictive than others is inconclusive. In our own research, as reported earlier, we uncovered numerous instances of labour conflict and labour resistance, but these were common across both Chinese and non-Chinese manufacturing firms. Many Chinese managers report that the labour conflicts they are involved in

---

[40] Interviewed in Chinese-owned factory in Ethiopia, July 2018.

reflect initial tensions commonly found in countries embarking on the path to industrialization, especially those arising from workers with no factory experience encountering Asian industrial work cultures (Tang and Eom 2019). Indeed, as this subsection shows, labour resistance is far more common than usually recognized in early stages of industrialization, both in early industrializer and in late industrializer experiences.

A common concern following the arrival of new investors to industrial parks such as Hawassa in Ethiopia has been the high labour turnover experienced by most factories employing young rural women taking on their first stable job. Absenteeism has also been widely reported as a serious problem, especially in the early stages of operations and for new workers lacking factory work experience (Gebrechristos 2025). High labour turnover and absenteeism are expressions of labour resistance, driven by workers' struggles to adapt to a new work culture, an industrial capitalist culture, especially in contrast to the different rhythms of agricultural work. Such struggles and forms of resistance are well established in the long history of industrial capitalism. A cursory look at the literature on both early and late industrialization, along with classic works about the building of an industrial workforce, yields myriad examples, with labour turnover just one of many forms of resistance, albeit a prevalent one (Thompson 1967; Ong 1987; Oya 2019; Mokyr and Voth 2010).[41] Other well-known forms on non-organized resistance also include individual acts of defiance, like slowing down the pace of work, or sabotage, theft, and improvised ('wildcat) strikes, instances of which we also found in our surveys in Angola and Ethiopia.

Economic historians of Africa have also documented the difficulties capitalist employers have faced in recruiting, retaining, and disciplining workers, whether in plantations, mines, or construction projects (Cooper 1992). In contemporary Ethiopia, as well as other African countries playing host to new, globally integrated factories, what many (managers, workers, observers) perceive as a clash of 'cultures' – hardworking Chinese 'eating bitterness' vs inefficient African workers resistant to long hours and strenuous factory rhythms – is in fact a vivid expression of the clash between the modern industrial capitalist work culture and that of low-productivity small-scale agriculture (Sun 2017; Oya 2019; Tang and Eom 2019).[42]

---

[41] This paragraph owes much to an excellent online essay written by Pseudoeramus, a global economic historian writing under a pseudonym who dissects a voluminous literature to produce a fascinating account detailing manifestations of labour resistance and labour repression, as well as variations among early industrializers, through an empirically grounded contrast between cotton mills in Japan and India in the nineteenth and early twentieth centuries https://pseudoerasmus.com/2017/10/02/ijd/.

[42] 'Culturalist' explanations are common in such situations. Chang (2008) provides many examples of historical stereotypes that run counter to contemporary ones, for example, the 'lazy Japanese', or when Confucian culture was regarded as inimical to material progress.

This clash has played out since the origin of capitalism over 200 years ago and has often been resolved through the establishment of new labour control mechanisms, such as worker dormitories (Tsurumi 1990; Pun and Smith 2007).

Hardy and Hauge (2019) point to low wages, hazardous conditions, and lack of agency as key drivers of labour turnover and mismatched expectations in Ethiopia's foreign-owned factories. The same study also shows that companies have been prepared to make some concessions and improve working conditions, although wages tend to be the lowest placed item on the agenda. The current reluctance to stay in factory employment expressed by many women in Ethiopia's garment factories is, however, also a reflection of the fact that factory jobs have to compete with alternative livelihoods in the form of international migration, self-employment (micro-business), returning to the village of origin, wage work in informal services, or even temporary reliance on relatives (World Bank 2016). Although these might not represent better alternatives in terms of returns on labour and earning stability, they nevertheless offer escape routes from the disappointment and frustration provoked by mismatched expectations. Such obstacles can be seen to have slowed down the scaling up of manufacturing in earlier historical examples – for example, India when compared to Japan in the same period (Otsuka et al. 1988). The documentary *Made in Ethiopia* lays bare these contradictions among contemporary women factory workers in Ethiopia, even if the main character Beti eventually opts to remain in factory work due to the alternatives being insufficient for survival.[43] Beti's predicament also points to the potentially emancipatory nature of stable salaried industrial employment for women seeking to escape patriarchy and systemic vulnerability (Kabeer 2024).

Once in the job, resistance to factory discipline is common among workers in early industrialization, especially concerning changes in work regimes or technological advances that might weaken workers' structural bargaining power. Bargaining over wages, effort at a given wage, and how many machines workers have to operate are critical for productivity growth, scaling up, employment dynamics, and work condition outcomes over time (Broadberry et al. 2015). In this respect, conflicts over effort, time, and wages have been at the heart of the textile and apparel industry ever since cotton mills became the engine driving the emergence of industrial capitalism (Freeman 2018), and through successive waves of expansion into late developers such as Japan, India, Korea, China, Bangladesh, and now Ethiopia. As far back as nineteenth-century Britain, many rural workers struggled to adapt to the precision and

---

[43] *Made in Ethiopia*, by Max Duncan and Xinyan Yu https://youtu.be/rnINvliEKes?si=iLW9Dr_FhQEBYugU.

discipline required in textile mills, leading to workplace tensions over efficiency imperatives and the adoption of new working methods or technology (Thompson 1967; Mokyr and Voth 2010).

Virtually all countries seeking to industrialize and build an industrial workforce go through the textile and apparel stage and the labour process dynamics specific to this industry, inevitably characterized by a particularly tough work environment (Brooks 2019). This does not mean the factories of the present are necessarily as bad as the sweatshops of the past (Mezzadri 2016). Conditions also change over time. The Ethiopian government has been particularly adamant about industrial parks having high-quality conditions in terms of space, ventilation, clean water, health and safety, environmental standards, and other basic amenities (Oqubay 2020). As previously mentioned, there has also been resistance to the idea of work dormitories, which some have seen as a marker of China's industrial relations in export-oriented regions, where such institutional mechanisms are used to enhance labour control over migrant workers (Pun and Smith 2007). Thus, conditions and social upgrading are ultimately the outcome of contestation on the part of workers and their organizations, and governments aiming for a particular 'model'.

Even the process of unionization on the factory floor is highly contested. In Ethiopia's industrial parks, unions were initially discouraged and replaced by largely ineffective 'workers councils'. This approach was reversed a few years later in response to a wave of wildcat strikes and significant worker mobilization, which had political connotations (Oya and Schaefer 2021; Gebrechristos 2025). Thus, exit – in the form of labour turnover – is not the only source of labour resistance or contestation. Lauria (2023), writing on road workers in Chinese projects, found that Ethiopian workers quickly discovered ways of peacefully but robustly confronting their Chinese managers arguing for wage increases, improvements in working conditions and financial rewards with often positive outcomes.

The frequency of factory strikes also shifts over time. In Ethiopia they increased substantially during the period 2016–2018, coinciding with the setting up of new industrial parks, the arrival of a wave of foreign investors, and a turbulent political period. Our 2017 worker survey indicated 38 per cent of factory workers had witnessed a strike in the previous 12 months, while a 2016 ILO survey reported 20 per cent of textile and garment firms had experienced one or more strikes over the preceding 12 months (Oya and Schaefer 2021). Wildcat strikes grew rapidly between the mid-2010s and the end of the decade across different sectors in Ethiopia, especially in industrial parks (Admasie 2022). Other studies report a continuous, although declining, incidence of strikes in industrial parks during 2019–2022, a period when grievances and disputes reported to park labour units increased, suggesting more institutionalized and progressively better managed labour conflict (Gebrechristos 2025, 206). A key lesson from these experiences is that – as demonstrated by the history of capitalism – factories, whether owned by Chinese or other employers, are excellent breeding grounds for labour mobilization and association.

Overall, what we observed in Ethiopia's textile and apparel industry is remarkably reminiscent of early industrialization experiences in multiple contexts, from Britain to India, Japan, and Mexico (Otsuka et al. 1988; Tsurumi 1990; Galvarriato 2017). Four remarkable parallels stand out: (a) labour resistance in the form of lower work effort (non-acceptance of overtime work) and high turnover; (b) labour conflict in the form of unorganized strikes; (c) late arrival of unions to stabilize the situation after initial resistance to unionization; and (d) new labour control mechanisms and labour repression to address these problems. Obstacles stemming from the labour market, as well as the extent to which the nature of the labour force hinders or accelerates industrial transformation, are central aspects of the economic development process – hence the need to centre the analysis in labour dynamics. The other key aspect is policy and politics, to which we now turn.

4 Policy, Politics, and Agency: Mediating the Impact of China on Africa's Industrialization

4.1 Agency, Policy, and Politics

Through contrasting Ethiopia and Angola as illustrative examples of variation in African experiences, this section examines the degree to which critical national institutions have emerged to pursue industrialization efforts and the political settlements associated with them. Here, a focus on critical infrastructure and FDI management provides a useful lens with which to make sense of their variegated outcomes found in the two countries. The shifting nature of state–business relations involving African states and Chinese capital, especially at times of significant disruption (economic crisis, pandemic, conflict) will also be discussed, taking into consideration the particularities of sectors, varieties of capital, and national/local political economy factors.

'Agency' is increasingly evoked in contemporary debates about China in Africa (Mohan and Lampert 2013), but does not constitute a particularly useful term if used vaguely. Large (2021) provides a compelling assessment of the pros and cons of the concept and its uses. It is often framed in terms of the 'plan' (or lack of) for engagement with China being pursued by African countries – in other words, whether there is a vision for what they want to get out of this relationship, and what might be done to maximize its benefits (Soulé 2022). This is a normative use of the term, which may have a political rendering when framed in the context of African emancipation (Large 2021, 34). Agency can mean many different things, however, depending on its empirical manifestations and which player we choose to focus our attention on. Corkin (2013), for example, presents an empirically grounded account of the agency of Angolan political elites in shaping relations with China, especially when it comes to leveraging the enormous volume of finance as part of their state (re)building project. African state agency is also reflected in construction contracts and how they evolve. For example, in Zambia, a single-source requirement eventually gave way to institutionalized bidding among Chinese contractors in Zambia (Lee 2017, 56), while in Angola, a stipulation was made that at least 30 per cent of subcontracting go to local companies in projects financed by the country's 2016 credit line (Wanda et al. 2023).

While it is unsurprising that African governments and elites tend to be the focus of 'African agency' analyses, firms and entrepreneurs, civil society organizations (CSOs), trade unions, workers, and other constituencies also represent significant sources of cooperation and bargaining, or alternatively resistance and friction. Agency encompasses contestation, which often happens from below, when workers confront employers or CSOs challenge the state and its allies by seizing 'moments' for mobilization and resistance (Lee 2017; Oya and Schaefer 2021). The manner in which diverse sources of agency are arranged at different levels – from the workplace to the ministry to the international forum – ultimately shapes how interests are manifested, and in turn bargaining outcomes over finance, infrastructure projects, investment decisions, production processes, and workplace encounters. Broadly speaking, this Element touches on two manifestations of agency: bargaining and contestation, involving both state and non-state actors (especially workers, as illustrated in the previous section). More specifically, this section focuses primarily on state actors, domestic elites and varieties of capital, arguing that a clearer understanding of how diverse forms of agency are configured can help explain the 'politics of production' underpinning variations in China's encounters with different African countries.

Politics is indeed at the heart of 'agency'. Lee (2017, 158) concludes her book with the observation that 'it is politics – and more precisely, the political synergy between state and society – not bureaucracy or technocracy, that is the key to leveraging Chinese state capital for development'. Grasping the 'politics of production' in terms of its macro political and economic context, national institutions, policy drivers and balance of power is critical to uncovering variations in structural transformation trajectories, including the obstacles countries find along the way (Burawoy 1985). The costs of transitioning to political settlements more conducive to industrialization and dynamic structural transformation rest on the existing balance of power, how it evolves, and the capabilities of those organizations that are in a position to hinder or promote such a transition (Khan 2018). Large (2021, 107) concludes that, despite China's potential contributions to economic transformation processes, 'Politics continued to represent a fundamental challenge to Africa's structural transformation'. Ethiopia's tumultuous period of 2020–2024 is a good example in this regard, as explained next. Chinese managers and officials interviewed during our fieldwork frequently highlighted political obstacles, such as unresponsive bureaucracies or cumbersome, unclear regulations. Of particular concern, however, was the lack of political stability and policy continuity, either due to internal conflicts or simply a change in the ruling party following elections, a point also stressed by Large (2021).

Thus, analysing whether 'effective' (industrial) policies have been designed and implemented is not enough. Also needed is knowledge of the underlying political dynamics, and the extent to which they have enabled or hindered processes and outcomes. Development policy in many African countries is driven by a combination of internal politics – including complex relations between elite factions, as well as instances of state–society synergy or contestation – and structural extraversion, which often reduces the policy space for long-term industrialization planning. This may partially explain the paucity of Asian-style industrial strategies in evidence across SSA. Put another way, the local, national, and global political configurations affecting Africa means the industrialization path taken by the continent's countries may differ from that taken by other latecomers, China included (Sun 2017). Equally, some expressions of structural determinism in world systems or dependency theory fail to acknowledge shifting domestic politics and balances of power, which may challenge extraversion logics and push countries towards a more coherent long-term vision that does not require 'delinking' from the world system (Amsden 1979 and 2001).

With regards to agency, a key question is agency *for what* and *through which mechanisms*. Ethiopia offers one of the best examples of agency deployed in the service of an effective industrialization strategy. Starting in the early 2000s, securing policy space for alternative development strategies and learning from a wider set of experiences became key priorities for late Ethiopian prime minister Meles Zenawi, with these principles eventually applied to Ethiopia's 2010–2020 pursuit of a long-term industrial strategy (de Waal 2013; Cheru and Oqubay 2019). Loss of policy space, especially for homegrown industrial development, was indeed one of the most pernicious effects of aid dependence and Washington/post–Washington Consensus policies since the 1980s (Chang 2008). Against this backdrop, Zenawi's ambition, optimism, and aspiration to become a developmental state (de Waal 20132; Chang and Hauge 2019) bear echoes of Hirschman's 'possibilism' (Cramer et al. 2020).

China offers contemporary examples of such bold aspirations. For instance, the ambitious Made in China 2025 project – designed to place the country at the forefront of new green transition sectors, as well as achieve more presence in strategic semiconductor production – has achieved its core targets ahead of time, raising the prospect of China further expanding its share of global manufacturing by 2030 (UNIDO 2024). Such programmes require what Mazzucato (2021) calls 'mission', which translates into a vision of economic transformation supported by a set of key operational goals, policy mechanisms, institutions, and actors ready to contribute to it. History backs this up, demonstrating that the drive shown by a powerful, resource-equipped state to shift towards new strategic sectors is a critical ingredient. Needless to say, agency can also be used to pursue undesirable aims, such as the enrichment of a narrow elite faction, or to pursue a political agenda with no defined development objective (Soares de Oliveira 2015; Taylor 2019; Large 2021).

Before moving on to the differing industrial policy approaches of Ethiopia and Angola, it is worth noting a particularity of these and other recent African policy experiences, namely that Chinese actors – whether government organizations, lenders, SOE or other business – have refrained from providing African governments with policy blueprints, recommendations, technical advice or policy conditions. This is in contrast to the approach taken by many Western donors over the past three decades and despite the growing narrative of 'industrial cooperation' discussed in Section 2. Chinese authorities often stress the need for African countries to find their own path, and will only advance 'advice' in the form of its own historical example or direct forms of support to existing industrial strategies – for example, building critical economic infrastructure or encouraging the setting up of SEZs (i.e. concrete actions rather than documents).

4.2 Two Tales of Industrial Policy

Throughout, this Element has emphasized the importance of variations in experiences and outcomes, together with the need to transcend both methodological nationalism and Africa essentialism. Here, we briefly contrast the industrial policy experiences of Angola and Ethiopia – where Chinese engagement has been particularly strong – in order to illustrate how differences in policy agendas and actions are key to understanding, first, the variation found in recent industrialization experiences, and, second, the variegated effects of China's contributions to Africa's industrialization.

4.2.1 Ethiopia's Industrial Strategy

Although the Ethiopian government had already begun articulating a pro-industrialization vision from the early 2000s, it was the key period of 2010–2018 when the main ingredients for an industrial strategy were put in place via two five-year plans: GTP1 and GTP2. Multiple policy instruments, institutional mechanisms and coordination actions were gradually introduced over time, as described by Oqubay (2019), Cheru and Oqubay (2019), Chang and Hauge (2019), Mamo (2024) and Hauge (2019). The Ethiopian government, following the example of many late industrializers, combined ISI and EOI approaches according to sectoral capabilities. ISI measures were primarily dedicated to building materials (cement, steel), food processing and, to a lesser extent, pharmaceuticals, while the EOI measures focused on textile and apparel, leather products, and floriculture. This combination in theory allowed for the promotion of inter-sector linkages, following Hirschman's typology.

The government's key industrial policy mechanisms included (Oqubay 2019): (a) dedicated industrial finance through the deployment of state development banks; (b) a vast expansion in basic infrastructure, particularly in power generation and transmission, connectivity (road, railway, logistics and dry port), and industrial park construction; (c) FDI promotion through various incentives, targeted at particular manufacturing sectors; (d) industrial park development (and setting up of SOEs to manage industrial parks) to house new investors, usually 'specialized' and clustered by manufacturing activity sub-sector; (e) trade policy and protection, including tariffs for ISI sectors (building materials), and export bans and controls to promote processing; (f) leverage of trade preferences (e.g. AGOA) to access the US market and provide additional incentives for Asian suppliers specializing in the US apparel market; (g) SOE deployment in strategic areas, especially construction, cement, textiles, logistics and industrial park development; (h) sector-related agencies for learning and support; and (i) macroeconomic measures, essentially targeting foreign exchange access and currency exchange rates. Looking at this list, it is hard to ignore the Asian influence.

During 2005–2018, and especially after 2012, a number of factors proved key to furthering the Ethiopian government's ambitious goals and making the mechanisms listed earlier more effective:[44] (a) a conducive political settlement,

---

[44] Many of this subsection's insights are drawn from IDCEA qualitative interviews conducted in 2016–2018.

with strong central leadership intent on solving common coordination failures; (b) the capacity to discipline sources of finance through national development banks and bargaining with donor agencies, including Chinese policy banks, with a view to steering funding towards priorities set out in operational plans (e.g. channelling domestic and external development finance towards industrial hubs and industrial development infrastructure); (c) a focus on ambitious employment and foreign exchange targets, while avoiding a 'race to the bottom' in the form of new 'sweatshops'; (d) a 'building verticality' approach, which involved persuading top-tier buyer brands (e.g. PvH, H&M) to source from Ethiopia and in doing so bring their supply chains with them, thereby attracting higher quality suppliers from Asia; and (e) the pursuit of policy learning and experimentation before and during the policy design, formulation and implementation process, including an unusual openness to recognizing mistakes (Oqubay 2019).

When it came to promoting light manufacturing, it was striking how Ethiopian delegations toured the world in order to learn from the successes and failures experienced in Asia, Latin America and Africa, especially in China, Vietnam, Singapore, and Mauritius around issues of FDI attraction and management, industrial hubs and SOEs (Oqubay 2015, 2022). Moreover, the 2012 success of Prime Minister Zenawi persuading a Chinese pioneer firm (Huajian) to take the lead in investing in a major shoe factory in the newly established EIZ was considered a turning point, and opened Ethiopia up to China's large private business interests (Oqubay and Lin 2019; Lin 2018). ISI-type industries such as cement were also thriving at the time, with domestic firms contributing to a large share of the rapid expansion in production. This was largely thanks to aggressive backward integration policies, including the banning of bagged cement imports (Whitfield and Zalk 2020).[45] The achievements of the Ethiopian government's approach during the 2010–2018 period are striking both in terms of manufacturing-value-added growth, attraction of manufacturing FDI, and the creation of tens of thousands of industrial jobs for Ethiopian youth.

It should be acknowledged, however, that not everything was rosy in Ethiopia's industrial strategy during this time, with several issues preventing an even greater level of success. First, and perhaps foremost, were the limited spillovers to the domestic manufacturing sector. Challenges in synergies between the country's infrastructure, logistics, urban development, and university and technical education systems impeded faster development of local

---

[45] A similar outcome was achieved in Nigeria, although with a less interventionist industrial policy (Wolf 2024).

industrial eco-systems around industrial parks, despite the Ethiopian state's considerable coordination efforts since 2015 (Oqubay 2022; Goodfellow and Huang 2022). As several studies of Chinese manufacturing investments in other countries have highlighted (Xia 2021; Tang 2020; Mamo 2024), this reflects structural infrastructure and industrial eco-system weaknesses common across most of Africa.

Initially at least, the limited spillovers in Ethiopia's industrial parks could also be ascribed to the types of GVCs/GPNs attracted to the country, especially the apparel sector, which is characterized by strong global competitive pressures, thin margins, limited room for manoeuvre, and persistent demands from global buyers to respond within tight time limits. Incorporating local suppliers and more local management representatives requires time, patience, and effort, potentially compromising these imperatives. Hence, the limited incentives for investors, including Chinese firms exporting to the United States and Europe, to proactively contribute to greater local spillovers. Moreover, given how fluid these investments were in a context of intense competition between countries looking to attract them, the Ethiopian government had its hands tied to some degree.

Hauge (2019) argues that Ethiopia failed to apply the kinds of reciprocal control mechanisms Korea and Taiwan used to discipline local and foreign capital (Amsden 2001). Unlike Ethiopia, Korea and Taiwan had an 'active state that pushed local content requirements and joint venture requirements on foreign investors', thereby contributing to important spillovers and backward linkages to domestic firms. This, Hauge (2019, 13) asserts, is something that Ethiopia has struggled to achieve due to the difficulties in attracting key industrial investors to industrial parks. There are, however, two issues with this rather pessimistic contrast. First, the Korean state was primarily focused on an emerging domestic industrial class, which was easier to discipline, whereas the Ethiopian state has more limited leverage over foreign investors with multiple production location options. Second, the industrial strategy implemented between 2016 and 2020 did contain both explicit and implicit reciprocal control mechanisms. Reliance on due diligence to target the most reliable investors was one way of reducing the need for discipline mechanisms. Furthermore, the Ethiopian government prioritized incentives that were directly linked to production, such as low electricity costs and facilitating the arrival of expat talent skilled in production management and setting up factories (Oqubay 2019 and 2022).

The government also imposed export targets, employing foreign exchange licences to push foreign firms to export more. The use of forex licences and linked export performance targets as a mechanism for creating learning rents was at least partly successful, driving some Chinese firms originally oriented towards the domestic market to export part of their production in order to access forex (Hauge 2019; Chen 2021). The Ethiopian government and its partners also showed themselves to be relatively agile and effective in managing the initial shock of the COVID-19 pandemic in 2020, saving thousands of jobs and helping firms stay afloat both through providing opportunities to repurpose for personal protective equipment (PPE) production and offering major discounts for trade logistics (Oqubay 2022; Gebrechristos 2025). Such measures induced resilience among foreign-owned, especially Chinese, manufacturing firms, which opted to maintain operations despite the impact of the pandemic and growing insecurity in the country.

Some may ask whether it was wise to place such focus on textile and apparel exporters. In this respect, Ethiopian policymakers were simply acknowledging the fact that the country has few real alternatives when it comes to generating sustained export revenue and employment from manufacturing production. Attempts were made to develop other sub-sectors through specialized industrial hubs – namely pharmaceutical, leather products and food processing – but without the success experienced in the textile and apparel sector. Given the severe foreign exchange constraints and serious employment challenges Ethiopia faced at the time, focusing on the emerging light manufacturing sector as a means of creating thousands of jobs for young women and men represented one of the few sensible options available at the time. Additionally, a lack of domestic industrial capabilities for export meant pursuing this path through FDI was also the only viable route. Besides, Ethiopia is far from exceptional in an African context, where countries often lack a domestic political lobby group willing to press for labour-intensive EOI in contrast to the effective rent-seeking support for capital-intensive ISI firms (Austin 2013).

Although the Ethiopian government had some success in pushing Chinese and other foreign firms to export more and reduce foreign exchange leakages, its power proved limited when trying to force them to invest in local supply chains still in their infancy. The relatively low quality of the local managerial workforce further reduced the incentive to localize and generate other spillovers in the short term, although measures have been put in place since 2018 to facilitate knowledge transmission and organizational capabilities through the hiring of local engineers and mid-level managers (Oya et al. 2022). Prior to the COVID-19 pandemic striking, the government agreed a plan with the Hawassa Industrial Park (HIP) Investors Association to nurture local managerial talent as incubators of small-scale accessory subcontractors ('spin-off' companies), which were to be located within the park and serve the main apparel exporters.[46] This required coordination between different government agencies, the

---

[46] Point made by former policymaker in interview dated 14 February 2025.

investors, Hawassa University, and local managers themselves. A HIP-based Chinese firm launched a recruitment campaign in Ethiopian higher education institutes specializing in textile engineering. The thirty individuals selected were then trained up, including through factory stays in China, in an effort to nurture local factory management capabilities. This planned approach took on board a key lesson from Asia: namely, that the active participation of domestic capital in industrial development processes – rather than a total reliance on foreign capital (FDI) – is critical, at least in the medium to long term (Amsden 2001).

The second issue relates to the fact that a critical ingredient of successful industrialization trajectories is the effective articulation of different levels of governance, particularly the division between central and subnational levels. China offers an excellent example, as 'directed improvisation' connecting the central and provincial/local levels made it possible to stick to critical top-down priorities while allowing space for local-level experimentation and learning-by-doing (Ang 2016).[47] Turning to Ethiopia, although HIP has often been regarded as a success story, the park has faced some difficult challenges, mostly stemming from inadequate articulation of the respective responsibilities of different governance levels. Although the federal level was very active in getting HIP up and running – with the EIC and IPDC successfully attracting and managing foreign investors – as well as coordinating efforts to manage the park and associated labour sourcing, teething problems swiftly emerged. These were linked to the very limited capacities of regional and local governments to, among other things, invest in local infrastructure, resolve local challenges, address housing shortages and manage land access (Goodfellow and Huang 2022; Mamo 2024; Gebrechristos 2025).

The third issue, which is directly associated with the second, concerns the difficulties for Ethiopia's industrial strategy to adequately manage labour – in other words, mobilize and incentivize workers to join industrial parks and remain in their jobs. As shown in Section 3, evidence of labour turnover, strikes and other forms of labour resistance suggests Ethiopia's incorporation into apparel GPNs has been fractious in the early stages (Hardy and Hauge 2019; Oya and Schaefer 2021; Gebrechristos 2025). Initial challenges faced by migrant workers in places like Hawassa, such as lack of affordable housing or sexual harassment while travelling to work, also reflect the difficult articulation between federal-level industrial policy imperatives and the realities of local-level state capacity in facilitating large labour transfers from rural areas to the

---

[47] See also Best (2018) on similar kinds of articulation in other successful industrial stories in Europe and the United States.

cities and towns neighbouring industrial parks (Ali 2024). The relatively high cost of housing rents, combined with low starting wages, fuelled discontent and turnover, as new workers expected a stable income that would allow them to live comfortably while sending remittances to their families. Admittedly, however, such issues are perhaps unsurprising in the context of accelerated workforce development during a period of rapid industrial development (Oya 2019; Gebrechristos 2025). Moreover, there is evidence that conditions gradually improved and labour turnover declined within a few years as core workforces stabilized, some companies adapted better to local conditions and to some demands from workers, and labour sourcing mechanisms became more effective through learning (Gebrechristos 2025).

To these three sets of issues, one can add such other shortcomings as inadequate management of revenue and customs; foreign exchange shortages (which have recently crippled the export-oriented manufacturing sector); and the disappointing performance of logistics for exports (Oqubay 2015; Mamo 2024). In some sub-sectors (e.g. leather), dedicated institutions have enjoyed only limited capacities with which to strengthen and discipline fragmented industries where incentives to export finished products are insufficient (Mamo 2024). Managing debt is another important policy challenge that recently became acute in some African countries, including Ethiopia, where the limited net foreign exchange generated by manufactured exports has been offset by growing levels of debt servicing. This is increasingly leading to serious foreign exchange shortages, further impeding economic growth and industrial development, a rather persistent problem in Ethiopia (Yimer and Geda 2024).

Finally, not every eventuality can be anticipated, with external dynamics and politics intervening to complicate success stories. Both Ethiopia and Angola – as elsewhere on the world – were severely impacted by the COVID pandemic, including the virtual 'closure' of China for two years. On top of this, civil war erupted in Ethiopia in November 2020. Oqubay (2019) and several other commentators (Clapham 2018) had already anticipated some of the political tensions and threats arising from both outside and within the Ethiopian People's Revolutionary Democratic Front (EPRDF) regime, with unrest, factionalism, and tensions over federalism, ethnic claims and regional politics already apparent as far back as the 2005 elections. One of the most damaging effects of the civil war on the apparel sector was arguably the suspension of AGOA trade preferences in the USA due to sanctions connected to the conflict. Without AGOA, many of the investors in Ethiopia exporting to US markets lost a key incentive to stay or invest in the country, despite the fact that since 2017 Ethiopia had become the second largest destination for FDI in textile and apparel after Vietnam.

Despite these challenges, a remarkable feature of many Chinese and some other foreign manufacturing firms has been their resilience and adaptability in the face of such adversity, whether repurposing to produce facemasks during the pandemic, reorienting production to local markets, or seeking out new external markets and buyers after AGOA was suspended. An export market diversification strategy is likely to become imperative given scant chances that AGOA will be extended under Trump administration. This resilience was partly induced by concerted government action aimed at protecting industrial investors and jobs, as well as persistent confidence among several investors that any political instability will be temporary (Oya and Schaefer 2024; Gebrechristos 2025). At the time of writing (2025), the number of Chinese firms in the EIZ had actually increased compared to 2018.[48] Nevertheless, the security situation is yet to be fully resolved, with the more fragile political settlement that is emerging potentially putting the brakes on the rapid industrialization drive initiated in the early 2010s, regardless of China's ongoing engagements (Lavers 2023).

Most of the challenges Ethiopia has faced are, however, fairly standard in early stages of industrialization. History teaches us that even the most successful industrialization stories in Asia and elsewhere were peppered with failures and took decades to come to fruition (Amsden 2001; Chang 2008; Oqubay 2020). Overall, Ethiopia's contemporary experience with industrial policy is remarkable for the comprehensive multipronged approach adopted, as well as the speed with which various measures, organizations, and institutional mechanisms have been established and operationalized. While such ambition and pace inevitably involve costs, mistakes, and obstacles, it is – following Hirschman's principle of the 'hiding hand' – precisely this determination and risk-taking that has yielded the best opportunities for policy learning in action (Hirschman 1967; Cramer et al. 2020). Africa's current era of industrial policy revival (UNECA 2016) has seen several countries (including Nigeria, Ghana, Kenya, Rwanda, Benin, Tanzania) put in place at least some of the measures Ethiopia has implemented, either to nurture particular domestic-oriented industries or to promote specific light manufacturing activities for export. No other African country in recent times, however, has pursued such a comprehensive policy approach nor achieved comparable results to these achieved by Ethiopia in the period 2015–2020. One can only speculate about the astonishing manufacturing growth Ethiopia might have achieved in the full ten years since 2015 had the post-2020 upheavals not occurred.

---

[48] Key informant from the EIZ, February 2025.

4.2.2 Angola's (Lack of) Industrial Strategy

Compared to Ethiopia, not nearly as much can be said about Angola's industrial policy, as during our research it barely existed in any coherent form.[49] In fact, while there is evidence of public investment and measures promoting industrialization, Angola's industrial policy consists of little more than disjointed, half-hearted efforts taking place amid myriad contradictions. It is true that since the end of the country's civil war in 2002, the Angolan government has often proclaimed the imperative of economic diversification. This had been reflected in multiple policy proclamations, with the National Development Plan 2013–2017 (NDP 2013–2017) and its successor, the National Development Plan 2018–2022 (NDP 2018–2022), emphasizing the need for labour-intensive industries at a time when youth employment challenges had started to degrade the legitimacy of the regime (Wanda 2021).

In 2015, Angola emerged from a commodity boom, with the effects of the oil price crisis felt throughout the economy. The country's lack of diversification and excessive dependence on imports for too many goods reinvigorated calls for economic transformation, albeit at a time when the government had limited resources to invest. Opportunities had arguably been missed during the years of the commodity boom, especially 2005–2015, when the availability of Chinese finance and high oil rents provided the conditions for vast reinvestment in other productive sectors. During the bonanza, the construction sector benefitted from the country's vast reconstruction programme, real estate developers throve, and importers and retailers were quick to join the party. At the same time, the manufacturing sector struggled to compete with (mostly Chinese) imports or obtain support from the state, despite some respectable growth until 2014 (albeit from a very low base).

The most important phenomenon affecting Angola's prospects for industrialization was the post-war infrastructure construction boom, which unsurprisingly led to great demand for inputs and materials required by the construction sector. As argued in Section 2, as an example of demand-induced investment dynamics (Hirschman 1958), the rise of construction material imports signalled a market opportunity for profitable manufacturing, especially given expectations of a prolonged infrastructure and real estate boom, resulting in impetus for the domestically oriented building materials sector, especially local cement production (Wolf 2017 and 2024; Ovadia 2018; Wanda 2021). Just as textiles has acted as a springboard for manufactured exports in many countries, so

---

[49] Much of the material in this section is based on direct IDCEA interviews conducted between 2016 and 2018 with government officials, business people, industry experts, and representatives of international agencies operating in Angola.

cement production has been used by several Asian countries 'as a springboard for industrialization and to develop technological capabilities within local firms, including professional management skills' (Whitfield and Zalk 2020, 848; see also Amsden, 1985 on Taiwan). The fact that cement is less likely to be internationally traded increases the viability of new production plants, despite the high costs involved. Nevertheless, promotion of this sector in Angola may not have happened without the direct involvement of leading figures in the President Dos Santos network, who were major investors in the two largest cement plants, one of which was co-owned and managed by a private Chinese company (CIF). The growing interest of Angolan business-political elites in construction goods manufacturing indicates 'there is more to the Angolan elite than their rent-seeking behaviour' (Ovadia 2018, 602). Wanda (2021) raises the question of why they invested in cement rather than stick to the low-risk, high-returns rewards offered by finance or resource extraction. Wolf (2024) suggests the involvement of local political-business elites in the building materials sector is not a unique phenomenon and in fact is increasingly common across industrialization efforts in Africa, with Nigeria and Ethiopia both having experienced a rapid expansion of their cement and steel industries. Chinese firms – a mix of translocal migrant entrepreneurs and large companies such as CITIC and CIF – have also placed their bets in the building materials sector, especially after 2014.

These positive developments cannot, however, be traced to the implementation of any coherent industrial policy package. In fact, in 2009, during the initial stages of the reconstruction boom and amid a context of local industry having only limited production capacities, especially for key materials like cement, glass, and steel, the government removed import duties on several of these products. This was done in order to support contractors struggling to meet infrastructure project deadlines due to lack of materials or overly expensive imports (Corkin 2013; Soares de Oliveira 2015). Chinese contractors in particular were accused by local industry lobbies of applying pressure aimed at liberalizing imports, despite numerous domestic and other foreign contractors also benefiting from lower-cost imports. In short, Angola's government could have taken advantage of this crucial moment to support local industry in boosting its production capacity, allowing it to meet exploding internal demand, as happened in Ethiopia. Instead, it chose to do the opposite. In this instance, the interests of the increasingly influential construction business and the imperatives of delivering the country's reconstruction left little room for serious industrial policy thinking (Wanda 2021).

On the other hand, the Dos Santos regime was adamant about nurturing a 'national bourgeoisie' that could reduce external dependence and consolidate the growing links between the ruling party (the People's Movement for the Liberation of Angola, or MPLA), and the emerging capitalist class (Ovadia

2018; Wanda 2021). The question remained of what the quickest route to achieving this was. Initially, manufacturing did not feature highly in this regard, with Angola's primary sites of accumulation centred around resource extraction rents, the booming construction sector (infrastructure and real estate), oil services, and banking (Soares de Oliveira 2015; Pitcher 2017). The growth of domestic banking was particularly striking and echoed developments in Nigeria during its own resource boom and liberalization era (Ferreira and Soares de Oliveira 2019). Yet, as Wanda (2021) documents, 'party entrepreneurs' – a faction among Angolan army generals and within the broad MPLA coalition – *also* opted to participate in emerging industrial business, as part of diversified business group logics. Thus, regardless of Angola's incoherent industrial policy at the time, opportunities were seized and elements of a 'part-time' industrial bourgeoisie began to emerge.

Moreover, the lack of a comprehensive, overarching industrial policy did not prevent some notable attempts being made at practicing industrial policy. For example, Sonangol Industrial Investments[50] contributed to industrialization efforts through equity investments in several ISI sub-sectors, especially the promotion of a new industrial ISI-led SEZ located in Luanda-Bengo, where over fifty Sonangol-owned factories were established (later mostly privatized or shut down). The SEZ survived despite long delays in its implementation and sluggish take-up from foreign and local business (with the exception of a Chinese SOE-owned aluminium plant), appearing to contribute to some of the industrial recovery experienced until 2015 (Ovadia 2018). Based on research conducted years later, however, Lippolis (2022) argues that this industrial policy experiment was in fact a massive failure, demonstrating why such initiatives so often fail to deliver the public goods needed for eventual industrial take-off. In this case, the policy ended up reproducing rent-seeking dynamics and was used as an instrument for enforcing cohesion in the MPLA party-state. In other words, it cannot really be seen as a form of 'developmental patrimonialism' (Kelsall 2013).

Local content policy offers another example of the incoherence at the heart of Angola's industrial policy: present in the country for decades, it was expected to be a vehicle for diversification and the development of construction sector-linked domestic industrial capabilities. Here, Corkin (2013, 184) notes that 'despite a body of local content laws, there are several notable examples of the contradicting policy environment present in Angola, whereby short-term gain is prioritized above local content development'. Although companies were set performance

---

[50] Sonangol is Angola's main national oil company and the engine driving much of the country's business across various sectors.

criteria, inadequate state support was provided to ensure they were met, meaning local content could not be enforced. A critical issue in the Angolan government's approach has been its failure to implement in practice the myriad strategies and policies it produces (Corkin 2013; Lippolis 2022).

During our research process in 2015–2018, when the government seemed keen to diversify towards manufacturing, we saw no evidence of it setting explicit targets for the emerging manufacturing class. While the AIA – a lobby association representing the interests of Angolan and Portuguese manufacturers – managed to push the government into raising tariffs on imported building materials after years of liberalization, manufacturing companies seldom received any indication of the state's intended targets. Rather, the market was left to determine these needs, despite being on its knees due to the post-2015 economic crisis. Often, bargaining concerned whether certain construction companies, especially Chinese firms, had circumvented local suppliers through setting up their own construction material plants (such as CITIC's aluminium plant) or building their own local supply chains via Luanda's Chinese business diaspora. At the same time, Chinese industrial business networks lobbied the Angolan government or political elite factions to secure sourcing contracts. In other words, lobbying was largely limited to who got what share of the local market.

Ultimately, the main problem facing Angola during the Dos Santos era was the absence of a sustained, coherent industrial strategy focused on coordination and multiple complementary fronts. Instead, what prevailed was a disconnected series of discrete interventions – from an expensive new SEZ to ad hoc local content policy shifts, to providing political-business elites with soft credit in order to secure participation in lucrative industrial ventures like cement production – driven by circumstances and specific lobby groups. Although some degree of industrialization did occur in the building materials sector, this was despite rather than because of any comprehensive industrial strategy. The outcome was modest industrial development concentrated in few sub-sectors (building materials, some agro-processing and beverages), propelled mainly by market forces, selected MPLA 'party entrepreneurs' and a few foreign (especially Chinese) investors, including translocal migrant entrepreneurs. By contrast, and even allowing for its shortcomings, Ethiopia's experience was much closer to the compressed development-era Asian industrialization model.

4.3 Leveraging 'Global China' for Industrialization: Policy Imperatives or the Art of the Possible

The apparent revival of industrial policy across Africa over the past two decades has coincided with China's growing engagements with the continent. The preceding history of half-hearted industrialization attempts by African governments, lack of continuity, coordination failures, political obstacles, external hindrance, and weak capacities also offers important lessons for current efforts to industrialize (Chitonge and Lawrence 2020).

Understanding whether African governments are serious in their pursuit of credible, ambitious industrialization strategies necessitates close inspection of industrial policy politics and the gap between rhetoric and reality (Whitfield and Zalk 2020). The task of industrialization requires a favourable political settlement and balance of power conducive to dynamic accumulation and investment directed towards manufacturing, sometimes at the expense of other sectors and interests – hence a deeply political problem (Amsden 2001; Khan 2018; Chang and Hauge 2019; Opalo 2024). These conditions cannot be externally imposed or engineered, or copied from an existing 'ideal' model. Rather, what is needed is an organic co-evolution of states and markets, different institutions, global and local varieties of capital, and a clear articulation of the responsibilities held by different levels of governance (Ang 2016; Tang 2020). Ideas also matter, with the effective reality of policymaking influenced by whether policymakers have access to and adopt particular sets of ideas; whether individuals in powerful positions exercise agency to put in practice a given apparatus of ideas and aspirations; or whether a powerful organization embraces an ideological project (e.g. for or against neoliberalism) (Mukand and Rodrik 2018; Chang and Hauge 2019; Opalo 2024).

The contrast between Ethiopia and Angola underscores the aforementioned, while highlighting three other important stylized facts. First, ambition and 'possibilism' matter. To some extent, Ethiopia defied expectations given that its structural conditions at the time were not conducive to industrialization. Despite this, the government decided to bet on the possible advantages, persistently pursuing accelerated routes (primarily through FDI and dedicated infrastructure for industrial parks) as a means of fostering industrial development. Without the 'art of the possible', much of the industrial growth achieved by Ethiopia over the course of a single decade (2010–2020) would have been impossible. Second, the importance of policy learning and coordination – two critical ingredients emphasized by Amsden (2001), Hirschman (1967) and Chang (2008) – is demonstrated by their presence in Ethiopia's industrialization experience and absence in Angola's. Third, the management of FDI, whether in terms of attracting and selecting the right kind of investors or being able to discipline them into aligning their interests with national goals, is key. Although the case of Ethiopia highlights some of the difficulties that can arise in pursuing these goals, it also points to several mechanisms and institutions that can be of help. The case of Angola, meanwhile, shows that effective FDI management can only happen if the internal political settlement accedes to a developmental bargain with foreign capital, as opposed to the perpetuation of rentier politics, whereby foreign capital becomes a conduit for wealth accumulation among a narrow elite. Even in Angola's context, however, it is possible for domestic capital accumulation interests to exert a limited form of FDI management to 'pick winners', as in the cement industry.

Several policy implications can be drawn from these contrasting policy stories, as well as successes and failures elsewhere in Africa. In this respect, the absence of relevant policy imperatives in several African countries may go some way to explaining their limited industrialization achievements to date, despite potentially beneficial Chinese engagements.

First, several basic preconditions are required for any sustained industrial development. While there is no consensus on what the full list might look like, opinion has at least converged around two sets of factors: (a) good education and skills levels, whether high literacy rates (greater than 70 per cent) or a pool of potentially trainable workers with some relevant skills and experience (i.e. prior manufacturing experience); and (b) basic economic infrastructure, especially cheap, reliable electricity and logistics. Any industrial strategy should ensure these basic conditions are met and targeted towards the needs of sustained structural transformation.

Second, sources of capital matter, whether in the form of development finance to support infrastructure development and start-ups, or industrial capital (FDI) in contexts where the domestic industrial class is small or weak. Attracting long-term patient finance for structural transformation, alongside reliable foreign capital with embedded technology and suitable organizational capabilities, therefore constitutes another piece of the puzzle.

Third, state capabilities to reward learning while disciplining industrial capital to meet growth and innovation objectives – what Amsden (2001) calls 'reciprocal control mechanisms' – are needed to ensure adequate volumes of investment are directed at activities/uses conducive to sustained structural transformation. Different countries may have to experiment with different kinds of mechanisms, depending on the local context.

Fourth, measures should be put in place to facilitate and accelerate the building of an industrial workforce, whether by supporting mobility through more and better affordable housing and transport, or ensuring factory employers dedicate resources to continuous training and progressive career paths. In addition, history suggests that keeping unit labour costs competitive through productivity growth is more likely to achieve rapid economic and social upgrading than exercising wage restraint. As such, relying mostly on low wages to provide a competitive edge is unlikely to lead to sustainable outcomes.

Fifth, a stable macroeconomic environment is important, especially in terms of two basic indicators: (a) currency risk, with a competitive, stable exchange rate desirable; and (b) inflation, especially in terms of the prices for key wage goods such as food and accommodation, which are critical for a smooth transition of the emerging industrial labour force.

To be fully effective, many of the policy elements outlined earlier would need to be addressed as part of a comprehensive, coherent industrial policy package, which would provide strategic direction in terms of sectors to grow, investors to attract, and supporting mechanisms to be put in place (Cramer et al. 2020; Oqubay 2020; Tregenna 2023).

We therefore conclude the Element with a brief reflection on how agency and policy can translate China's multiple engagements in Africa into meaningful, sustained advances towards an industrial-led structural transformation. Throughout, this Element has argued that taking this path is imperative for most African countries seeking to exercise their 'right to development' and achieve meaningful progress when it comes to the welfare of their growing populations. The employment challenge is at the core of this imperative. As such, only a long-term, coherent, realistic strategy for mass job creation, alongside economic and social upgrading, can lead African countries to deserved prosperity. This is an aspiration that cannot be simply outsourced (Moore 2025).

At the same time, politics matters, complicating policymaking in ways that cannot always be easily predicted. Not all good things go together, and obstacles will inevitably appear on the road. Whether Chinese state or private investment – in all its manifestations – will enable African countries to achieve industrialization, thereby leaving behind the colonial legacy of primary commodity dependence, 'will depend on many factors beyond the volition of the Chinese state or African governments' (Lee 2017, 165).

China's dual image of being on the one hand a 'developing country' or 'country of the Global South',[51] and on the other an emerging global power challenging American hegemony, has implications for how 'African agency' is interpreted. Should agency be understood in terms of standing up to this emerging global power? Or is it about striking the best deal within a 'partnership of equals'? Regardless of rhetoric, it is clear that current power relations between China and African countries are shaping the likelihood of agency and nature of bargaining, with possible variations between African settings. The contrast between Angola and Ethiopia detailed in this section is

---

[51] These terms can be found in a number of Xi Jinping speeches, especially at the FOCAC 2024 Keynote address https://english.news.cn/20240905/e898a78004754f229763ad2bb5be7aa3/c.html.

illustrative of this divergence in relations and outcomes. The following oft-cited quote (Cramer et al. 2020, 143) from Hirschman (1967, 5) encapsulates the Element's proposed approach, which 'stresses the importance for development of what a country does and of what it becomes as a result of what it does, and thereby contests the primacy of what it is, that is, of its geography- and history-determined endowment with natural resources, values, institutions, social and political structure'.

Abbreviations

ADB	African Development Bank
AGOA	African Growth and Opportunity Act
CSO	civil society organization
EIC	Ethiopian Investment Commission
EIZ	Eastern Industrial Zone
EOI	export-oriented industrialization
EPC	engineering, procurement and construction
ETCDZ	economic and trade cooperation development zone
EV	electric vehicle
FDI	foreign direct investment
FOCAC	Forum on China–Africa Cooperation
GPN	global production network
GVC	global value chain
HIC	high-income country
HIP	Hawassa Industrial Park
IDCEA	Industrial Development Construction and Employment in Africa
ILO	International Labour Organization
IPDC	Ethiopian Industrial Parks Development Corporation
ISI	import substitution industrialization
LIC	low-income country
LMIC	low- and middle-income country
MPLA	People's Movement for the Liberation of Angola
NDRC	National Development and Reform Commission
SAP	structural adjustment programme
SEZ	special economic zone
SME	small and medium-sized enterprise
SSA	sub-Saharan Africa
SOE	state-owned enterprise
UNCTAD	UN Commission on Trade and Development

References

Ackah, C., Geda, A., Görg, H., & Merchan, F. (2024). What Role for Chinese FDI in Africa_ New Survey Evidence from Ethiopia and Ghana. *Kiel Working Paper, 2268.*

Acker, K., Brautigam, D., & Huang, Y. (2020). *Debt Relief with Chinese Characteristics*. Working Paper No. 2020/39. China Africa Research Initiative, School of Advanced International Studies, Johns Hopkins University, Washington, DC. www.sais-cari.org/publications.

Admasie, S. (2022). Ethiopia Shows 'Decline' of Unions to Be Greatly Exaggerated. Global Labour Column n. 422 https://globallabourcolumn.org.

Africa Confidential. (2024). Beijing's Green New Deal Pledges Factories in Africa. *Africa Confidential.*

African Development Bank. (ADB). (2018). *African Economic Outlook 2018*. African Development Bank.

Akamatsu, K. (1962) A Historical Pattern of Economic Growth in Developing Countries, *Developing Economies*, Tokyo, Preliminary Issue No. 1, pp. 3–25.

Akinrinade, S., & Ogen, O. (2008). Globalization and De-Industrialization: South-South Neo-liberalism and the Collapse of the Nigerian Textile Industry. *The Global South*, 2(2), 159–170.

Akorsu, A. D., & Cooke, F. L. (2011). Labour Standards Application among Chinese and Indian Firms in Ghana: Typical or Atypical? *The International Journal of Human Resource Management*, 22(13), 2730–2748.

Alden, C., & Lu, J. (2019). 'Brave New World: Debt, Industrialization and Security in China–Africa Relations. *International Affairs*, 95(3), 641–657. https://doi.org/10.1093/IA/IIZ083.

Ali, M. S. (2024). *The Political Economy of Apparel Exporting Industrial Parks in Ethiopia*. Cham: Palgrave Macmillan. https://doi.org/10.1007/978-3-031-60490-4.

Allen, R. C. (2011). *Global Economic History: A Very Short Introduction*. Oxford: Oxford University Press.

Amsden, A. (1979). Taiwan's Economic History: A Case of Etatisme and a Challenge to Dependency Theory. *Modern China*, 5(3), 341–379.

Amsden, A. H. (1985). The State and Economic Development in Taiwan. In P. Evans, D. Reuschemeyer, & T. Skocpol (Eds.), *Bringing the State Back in* (pp. 78–106). Cambridge: Cambridge University Press.

Amsden, A. H. (2001). *The Rise of 'the Rest': Challenges to the West from Late-Industrializing Economies*. Oxford: Oxford University Press.

References

Amsden, A. H. (2012). Grass Roots War on Poverty. *World Social and Economic Review*, 1, 114–131.

Andreoni, A., & Chang, H.-J. (2017). Bringing Production and Employment Back into Development: Alice Amsden's Legacy for a New Developmentalist Agenda. *Cambridge Journal of Regions, Economy and Society*, rsw029.

Ang, Y. Y. (2016) *How China Escaped the Poverty Trap*. Ithaca: Cornell University Press.

Anner, M. (2020). Squeezing Workers' Rights in Global Supply Chains: Purchasing Practices in the Bangladesh Garment Export Sector in Comparative Perspective. *Review of International Political Economy*, 27(2), 320–347.

Atkinson, R. D. (2024). *China Is Rapidly Becoming a Leading Innovator in Advanced Industries*. Information Technology and Innovation Foundation. www2.itif.org/2024-chinese-innovation-full-report.pdf.

Atta-Ankomah, R. (2016). Chinese Technologies and Pro-poor Industrialisation in Sub-Saharan Africa: The Case of Furniture Manufacturing in Kenya. *European Journal of Development Research*, 28, 397–413.

Austin, G. (2013). Labour-intensity and manufacturing in West Africa, c. 1450–c. 2000. In Austin, G. and K. Sugihara (eds.), *Labour-intensive industrialization in global history* (pp. 201–230). Abingdon: Routledge.

Baah, A. Y, & Jauch, H. (2009). *Chinese Investments in Africa: A Labour Perspective*. Accra: African Labour Research Network.

Balchin, N., Booth, D., & te Velde, D. W. (2019). *How Economic Transformation Happens at the Sector Level: Evidence from Africa and Asia*. London: ODI.

Bashir, S. (2015). *The Imperative of Skills Development for the Structural Transformation of Sub-Saharan Africa: Potential for China-World Bank-Africa Collaboration*. Partnering to Accelerate Investment, Industrialization, and Results in Africa, Addis Ababa.

Best, M. H. (2018). *How Growth Really Happens: The Making of Economic Miracles through Production, Governance, and Skills*. Princeton: Princeton University Press.

Brautigam, D. (2019). Chinese Loans and African Structural Transformation. In A. Oqubay & J. Y. Lin (Eds.), *China-Africa and an Economic Transformation* (pp. 129–146). Oxford: Oxford University Press.

Brautigam, D., & Rithmire, M. (2021). There Is No Chinese 'Debt Trap'. *The Atlantic*.

Brautigam, D., & Tang, X. (2014). 'Going Global in Groups': Structural Transformation and China's Special Economic Zones Overseas. *World Development*, 63, 78–91.

Brautigam, D., Tang, X., & Xia, Y. (2018). What Kinds of Chinese 'Geese' Are Flying to Africa? Evidence from Chinese Manufacturing Firms. *Journal of African Economies*, 27(suppl_1), i29–i51.

Brautigam, D., Diao, X., McMillan, M., & Silver J. (2019). *Chinese Investment in Africa: How Much Do We Know?* PEDL CEPR Synthesis Paper. https://pedl.cepr.org/publications/chinese-investment-africa-how-much-do-we-know.

Broadberry, S. N., Fukao, K., & Zammit, N. (2015). How Did Japan Catch-Up on the West? A Sectoral Analysis of Anglo-Japanese Productivity Differences, 1885–2000. CEPR Discussion Paper No. 10570.

Brooks, A. (2019). *Clothing Poverty: The Hidden World of Fast Fashion and Second-Hand Clothes*. London: Bloomsbury.

Burawoy, M. (1985). *The Politics of Production: Factory Regimes under Capitalism and Socialism*. London: Verso Books.

Calabrese, L., & Tang, X. (2023) Economic Transformation in Africa: What Is the Role of Chinese Firms? *Journal of International Development*, 35(1), 43–64.

Calabrese, L., Gelb, S., & Hou, J. (2017). *What Drives Chinese Outward Manufacturing Investment? A Review of Enabling Factors in Africa and Asia*. ODI-SET Background Paper, Overseas Development Institute, London.

Calderon, C., Cantu, C., & Chuhan-Pole, P. (2018). *Infrastructure Development in Sub-Saharan Africa: A Scorecard*. World Bank, Washington, DC. https://doi.org/10.1596/1813-9450-8425.

Chan, A. (2015). The Fallacy of Chinese Exceptionalism. In Chan, A. (Ed.), *Chinese Workers in Comparative Perspective*. Ithaca: Cornell University Press.

Chan, K. (2024). China's 'Overcapacity' Reveals Two Different Visions of the World. www.high-capacity.com/p/chinas-overcapacity-reveals-two-different.

Chang, D. (2022). Transnational Labour Regimes and Neo-liberal Development in Cambodia. *Journal of Contemporary Asia*, 52(1), 45–70. https://doi.org/10.1080/00472336.2020.1859122.

Chang, H. J. (2008). *Bad Samaritans: The Guilty Secrets of Rich Nations and the Threat to Global Prosperity*. New York: Random House.

Chang, H. J., & Andreoni, A. (2021). Bringing Production Back into Development: An Introduction. *European Journal of Development Research*, 33, 165–178.

Chang, H.-J., & Hauge, J. (2019). The Concept of a 'Developmental State' in Ethiopia. In F. Cheru, C. Cramer, & A. Oqubay (Eds.), *The Oxford Handbook of the Ethiopian Economy* (pp. 823–841). Oxford: Oxford University Press.

Chelwa, G. (2023). China and Africa's Industrialisation Attempts. *Wenhua Zongheng. Quarterly Journal of Chinese Thought*, 1(3), 7–12.

Chen, W. (2021). *The Dynamics of Chinese Private Outward Foreign Direct Investment in Ethiopia: A Comparison of the Light Manufacturing Industry and the Construction Materials Industry*. PhD thesis. SOAS University of London.

Chen, W. (2024). Heterogeneity and Drivers of Chinese Manufacturing FDI to Africa: Evidence from Angola and Ethiopia. IDCEA Working Paper n. 08. SOAS, London.

Chen, W., Dollar, D., & Tang, H. (2018). Why Is China Investing in Africa? Evidence from the Firm Level. *The World Bank Economic Review*, 32(3), 610–632.

Chen, Y. (2021). 'Africa's China': Chinese Manufacturing Investment in Nigeria and Channels for Technology Transfer. *Journal of Chinese Economic and Business Studies*, 19(4), 335–358.

Chen, Y. (2024). Technology Transfer on the Belt and Road: Pathways for Structural Transformation in Ethiopia's Standard Gauge Railways. *The European Journal of Development Research*, 36(3), 668–694.

Cheru, F., & Oqubay, A. (2019). Catalysing China–Africa Ties for Africa's Structural Transformation: Lessons from Ethiopia. In A. Oqubay & J. Y. Lin (Eds.), *China-Africa and an Economic Transformation* (1st ed., pp. 282–309). Oxford: Oxford University Press.

China-Africa Business Council (CABC). (2024). *China-Africa Investment Cooperation: A New Impetus to Africa's Industrialization*. China Africa Business Council.

Chitonge, H., & Lawrence, P. (2020). The Political Economy of Industrialization and Industrial Policy in Africa, 1960–2018. In A. Oqubay, C. Cramer, H. J. Chang, & R. Kozul-Wright (eds.), *The Oxford Handbook of Industrial Policy* (pp. 867–893). Oxford: Oxford University Press.

Chu, J., & Fafchamps, M. (2022). Labor Conflict within Foreign, Domestic, and Chinese-Owned Manufacturing Firms in Ethiopia. *World Development*, 159, 106037.

Clapham, C. S. (2018). The Ethiopian Developmental State. *Third World Quarterly*, 39(6), 1151–1165.

Cooper, F. (1992). Colonizing time: work rhythms and labor conflict in colonial Mombasa. In N. Dirks (ed.), *Colonialism and Culture*. Ann Arbor, MI: University of Michigan Press.

Corkin, L. (2012). Chinese Construction Companies in Angola: A Local Linkages Perspective. *Resources Policy*, 37(4), 475–483.

Corkin, L. (2013). *Uncovering African Agency: Angola's Management of China's Credit Lines*. London: Routledge.

Cramer, C., Sender, J., & Oqubay, A. (2020). *African Economic Development: Evidence, Theory, Policy*. Oxford: Oxford University Press.

Dappe, M. H., & Lebrand, M. (2024). Infrastructure and Structural Change in Africa. *The World Bank Economic Review*, 38(3), 483–513.

Darko, E. M., & Xu, K. (2024). The effect of Chinese foreign direct investment on Africa's industrialization process. *International Journal of Emerging Markets*, 19(10), 3139–3159.

de Waal, A. (2013). The theory and practice of Meles Zenawi. *African Affairs*, 112(446), 148–155.

Dethier, J. J. (2015). Infrastructure in Africa. In Monga C. & Lin, J.Y. (eds.), *The Oxford Handbook of Africa and Economics: Policies and Practices* (pp. 372–387). Oxford: Oxford University Press.

Development Reimagined (DR). (2024). *Transforming Africa into a Solar panel Manufacturing Hub with China's Support*. DRI. https://developmentreimagined.com/discussion-paper-transforming-africa-into-a-photovoltaic-manufacturing-hub-with-chinas-support-a-new-vision-for-sustainable-energy/.

Diao, X., Harttgen, K., & McMillan, M. (2017). The Changing Structure of Africa's Economies. *The World Bank Economic Review*, 31(2), 412–433.

Ellis, M., McMillan, M. S., & Sovani, M. (2021). *Labor-Related Knowledge Transfers from Chinese Foreign Direct Investment in Ethiopia and Tanzania*. International Food Policy Research Institute.

Engel, L., Hwang, J., Morro, D., & Bien-Aime, V. Y. (2024). Relative Risk and the Rate of Return. GCI Policy Brief 023. Boston University Global Development Policy Center.

Fei, D. (2020a). The Compound Labor Regime of Chinese Construction Projects in Ethiopia. *Geoforum*, 117, 13–23.

Fei, D. (2020b). Variegated Work Regimes of Chinese Investment in Ethiopia. *World Development*, 135, 105049.

Ferreira, M. E., & Soares De Oliveira, R. (2019). The Political Economy of Banking in Angola. *African Affairs*, 118(470), 49–74.

Franceschini, I., & Loubere, N. (2022). *Global China as Method* (1st ed.). Cambridge: Cambridge University Press.

Frazier, M. W. (2002). *The Making of the Chinese Industrial Workplace. State, Revolution, and Labour Management*. Cambridge: Cambridge University Press.

Freeman, J. B. (2018). *Behemoth: A History of the Factory and the Making of the Modern World*. New York: W. W. Norton and Co.

Gadzala, A. W. (2010). From Formal- to Informal-Sector Employment: Examining the Chinese Presence in Zambia. *Review of African Political Economy*, 37(123), 41–59.

Galvarriato, A. G. (2017). *Industria y revolución: cambio económico y social en el Valle de Orizaba, México*. Fondo de Cultura Económica.

Gambino, E., & Bagwandeen, M. (2024). A global sense of workplace: labour relations in Sino-African construction sites. In J. Hönke, E. Cezne, & Y. Yang (eds.), *Africa's Global Infrastructures: South-South Transformations in Practice* (pp. 204–233). London: Hurst Publishers.

Garlick, J., & Qin, F. (2024). China's 'do-as-I-do' Paradigm: Practice-Based Normative Diplomacy in the Global South. *The Pacific Review*, 37(5), 985–1015.

Gebrechristos, N. (2025). *Industrialisation and Workforce Development in Africa: Policy Dynamics, Firms, and Industrial Ecosystems*. Cham: Palgrave McMillan.

Geda, A., Senbet, L. W., & Simbanegavi, W. (2018). The Illusive Quest for Structural Transformation in Africa: Will China Make a Difference? *Journal of African Economies*, 27(suppl_1), i4–i14.

Giese, K., & Thiel, A. (2015). The Psychological Contract in Chinese-African Informal Labor Relations. *The International Journal of Human Resource Management*, 26(14), 1807–1826.

Goodfellow, T. (2020). Finance, infrastructure and urban capital: The political economy of African 'gap-filling'. *Review of African Political Economy*, 47(164), 256–274.

Goodfellow, T., & Huang, Z. (2022). Manufacturing Urbanism: Improvising the Urban–Industrial Nexus through Chinese Economic Zones in Africa. *Urban Studies*, 59(7), 1459–1480.

Gu, J., & Carey, R. (2019). China's Development Finance and African Infrastructure Development. In A. Oqubay, & J. Y. Lin (Eds.), *China-Africa and an Economic Transformation* (1st ed., pp. 147–172). Oxford: Oxford University Press.

Gutman J., & Zhang, C. (2015). Who Wins World Bank-Financed Government Contracts? June 24. Brookings www.brookings.edu/blog/africa-in-focus.

Haraguchi, N., Cheng, C. F. C., & Smeets, E. (2017). The Importance of Manufacturing in Economic Development: Has This Changed? *World Development*, 93, 293–315.

Hardy, V., & Hauge, J. (2019). Labour challenges in Ethiopia's textile and leather industries: no voice, no loyalty, no exit?. *African Affairs*, 118(473), 712–736.

Hauge, J. (2019). Should the African lion learn from the Asian tigers? A comparative-historical study of FDI-oriented industrial policy in Ethiopia, South Korea and Taiwan. *Third World Quarterly*, 40(11), 2071–2091.

Hauge, J. (2023). *The Future of The Factory*. Oxford: Oxford University Press.

Hirschman, A. O. (1958). *The Strategy of Economic Development*. New Haven: Yale University Press.

Hirschman, A. O. (1967). *Development Projects Observed*. Washington, DC: Brookings.

HRW. 2011. 'You'll Be Fired if You Refuse': Labor Abuses in Zambia's Chinese State-Owned Copper Mines. 3 November. www.hrw.org/reports/2011/11/03/you-ll-be-firedif-you-refuse.

Hung, H. (2008). Rise of China and the Global Overaccumulation Crisis. *Review of International Political Economy*, 15(2), 149–179.

IndustryALL. (2018). *Inditex _ IndustriALL Global Framework Agreement*. www.industriall-union.org/inditex.

Infrastructure Consortium for Africa (ICA). (2018). *Infrastructure Financing Trends in Africa - 2018. ICA Report 2018*. Abidjan: African Development Bank. www.icafrica.org/fileadmin/documents/IFT_2018/ICA_Infrastructure_Financing_in_Africa_Report_2018_En.pdf.

Inikori, J. E. (2020). Atlantic Slavery and the Rise of the Capitalist Global Economy. *Current Anthropology*, 61(S22), S159–S171.

International Labour Organization (ILO). (2019). *Advancing Social Justice: Shaping the future of work in Africa*. Geneva: ILO. https://www.ilo.org/sites/default/files/wcmsp5/groups/public/@ed_norm/@relconf/documents/meetingdocument/wcms_728052.pdf.

Itaman, R., & Wolf, C. (2021). Industrial policy and monopoly capitalism in Nigeria: Lessons from the Dangote Business Conglomerate. *Development and Change*, 52(6), 1473–1502.

Jenkins, R. (2019). *How China Is Reshaping the Global Economy*. Oxford: Oxford University Press.

Kabeer, N. (2024). *Renegotiating Patriarchy: Gender, Agency and the Bangladesh Paradox*. London: LSE Press.

Kaplinsky, R. (2008). What Does the Rise of China Do for Industrialisation in Sub-Saharan Africa? *Review of African Political Economy*, 35(115), 7–22.

Kelsall, D. T. (2013). *Business, Politics, and the State in Africa: Challenging the Orthodoxies on Growth and Transformation*. London: Zed Books.

Kenny, C., Duan, S., &Gehan, Z. (2025). Chinese Contractors and Development Project Quality. CGD Working Paper 715. Washington, DC: Center for Global Development. www.cgdev.org/publication/chinese-contractors-and-development-project-quality.

Khan, M. H. (2018). Political Settlements and the Analysis of Institutions. *African Affairs*, 117(469), 636–655.

Khan, M. H. (2019). Knowledge, Skills and Organizational Capabilities for Structural Transformation. *Structural Change and Economic Dynamics*, 48, 42–52.

Kibria, N. (1998). Becoming a Garments Worker: The Mobilization of Women into the Garments Factories of Bangladesh. UNRISD Occasional Paper No. 9, United Nations Research Institute for Social Development, Geneva.

Kopinski, D., & Carmody, P. (2023). The Political Economy of FDI and Spillovers in Africa: Can China Deliver on Hirschman's Ideas. In D. Kopiński, P. Carmody, & I. Taylor (Eds.), *The Political Economy of Chinese FDI and Spillover Effects in Africa* (pp. 15–45). Cham: Palgrave Macmillan.

Kruse, H., Mensah, E., Sen, K., & De Vries, G. (2023). A Manufacturing (Re)Naissance? Industrialization in the Developing World. *IMF Economic Review*, 71(2), 439–473.

Large, D. (2021). *China and Africa*. Cambridge: Polity.

Lavers, T. (2023). *Ethiopia's 'Developmental State': Political Order and Distributive Crisis*. Cambridge: Cambridge University Press.

Lee, C. K. (1999). From Organized Dependence to Disorganized Despotism: Changing Labour Regimes in Chinese Factories. *China Quarterly*, 157, 44–71.

Lee, C. K. (2017). *The Specter of Global China: Politics, Labor, and Foreign Investment in Africa*. Chicago: University of Chicago Press.

Lee, C. K. (2022). Global China at 20: Why, How and So What? *China Quarterly*, 250, 313–331.

Lerche, J., Mezzadri, A., Chang, D.O., et al. (2017). *The Triple Absence of Labour Rights: Triangular Labour Relations and Informalisation in the Construction and Garment Sectors in Delhi and Shanghai*. Centre for Development Policy and Research Working Paper 32/17, SOAS, University of London.

Li, W., & Lu, S. (2024). Assessing Structural Transformation and the Potential Impacts of Belt and Road Initiative Projects in Africa. *The European Journal of Development Research*, 36(3), 548–570.

Lippolis, N. (2022). The logic of authoritarian industrial policy: The case of Angola's special economic zone. *African Affairs*, 121(485), 595–622.

Lin, J. Y. (2018). China's Rise and Opportunity for Structural Transformation in Africa. *Journal of African Economies*, 27(suppl_1), i15–i28.

Lin, J., & Chang, H. J. (2009). Should Industrial Policy in Developing Countries Conform to Comparative Advantage or Defy It? A Debate between Justin Lin and Ha-Joon Chang. *Development policy review*, 27(5), 483–502.

Lin J. Y., & Wang, Y. (2017). *Going beyond Aid: Development Cooperation for Structural Transformation*. Cambridge: Cambridge University Press.

Lin, J. Y., & Xu, J. (2019). China's Light Manufacturing and Africa's Industrialization. In A. Oqubay & J. Y. Lin (Eds.), *China-Africa and an Economic Transformation* (1st ed., pp. 265–281). Oxford: Oxford University Press.

Lu, F., & Liu, X. (2018). Africa's Industrialization and China's OFDI in the Manufacturing Sector: Rationales and Practices. *China Economic Journal*, 11(2), 126–150.

Lüthje, B., Luo, S., & Zhang, H. (2013). *Beyond the Iron Rice Bowl: Regimes of Production and Industrial Relations in China*. Frankfurt: Campus Verlag.

Mackintosh, M., Banda, G., Tibandebage, P., & Wamae, W. (2015). *Making Medicines in Africa: The Political Economy of Industrializing for Local Health*. Cham: Palgrave Macmillan.

Mamo, A. H. (2024). *The Political Economy of Chinese FDI in Africa*. Cham: Palgrave Macmillan.

Mazzucato, M. (2021). *Mission economy: A moonshot guide to changing capitalism*. London: Penguin UK.

McKinsey. (2017). *Dance of the Lions and Dragons – How Are Africa and China Engaging, and How Will the Partnership Evolve?* McKinsey.

McKinsey. (2020). *Solving Africa's Infrastructure Paradox*. McKinsey.

McMillan, M., & Zeufack, A. (2022). Labor productivity Growth and Industrialization in Africa. *Journal of Economic Perspectives*, 36(1), 3–32.

McMillan, M., Rodrik, D., & Verduzco-Gallo, I. (2014). Globalization, Structural Change, and Productivity Growth, with an Update on Africa. *World Development*, 63, 11–32.

Meagher, K. (2016). The Scramble for Africans: Demography, Globalisation and Africa's Informal Labour Markets. *Journal of Development Studies*, 52(4), 483–497.

Megbowon, E., Mlambo, C., & Adekunle, B. (2019). Impact of China's Outward FDI on Sub-saharan Africa's Industrialization: Evidence from 26 Countries. *Cogent Economics & Finance*, 7(1), 1681054.

Mezzadri, A. (2016). *The Sweatshop Regime: Labouring Bodies, Exploitation and Garments 'Made in India'*. Cambridge: Cambridge University Press.

MFA China. (2024). *Forum on China-Africa Cooperation Beijing Action Plan (2025–2027)*. MFA-China.

Mkandawire, T. (1988). The Road to Crisis, Adjustment and De-industrialisation: The African Case. *Africa Development/Afrique et Développement*, 13(1), 5–31.

Mkandawire, T. (2005). African intellectuals and nationalism. In Mkandawire T. (ed.), *African intellectuals: Rethinking politics, language, gender and development* (pp. 10–53). London: Zed Books.

Mohan, G., & Lampert, B. (2013). Negotiating China: Reinserting African Agency into China–Africa relations. *African Affairs*, 112(446), 92–110.

Mokyr, J., & Voth, H. J. (2010). Understanding Growth in Europe, 1700–1870: Theory and Evidence Joel Mokyr and Hans-Joachim Voth. In S. Broadberry

& K. H. O'Rourke (Eds.), *The Cambridge Economic History of Modern Europe: Volume 1, 1700–1870*, 7 (pp. 7–42). Cambridge University Press.

Moore, W. G. (2025). Analysis: The Risk of Outsourcing Africa's Ambition. *Semafor*. www.semafor.com/article/01/13/2025/analysis-the-risk-of-outsourcing-ambition.

Morrissey, O. (2012). FDI in Sub-Saharan Africa: Few linkages, fewer spillovers. *The European Journal of Development Research*, 24(1), 26–31.

Moses, O., Ngui, D., Engel, L., & Kedir, A. (2024). *China-Africa Economic Bulletin, 2024 Edition*. Boston University Global Development Policy Center and African Economic Research Consortium.

Mukand, S., & Rodrik, D. (2018). *The Political Economy of Ideas: On Ideas Versus Interests in Policymaking*. NBER Working Paper No. w24467. National Bureau of Economic Research.

Newman, C., Page, J., Rand, J., et al. (Eds.). (2016). *Manufacturing Transformation: Comparative Studies of Industrial Development in Africa and Emerging Asia*. Oxford: Oxford University Press.

Nolan, P. (2014). *Chinese firms, global firms: Industrial policy in the age of globalization*. Abingdon: Routledge.

Ong, A. (1987). *Spirits of Resistance and Capitalist Discipline: Factory Women in Malaysia*. Albany: State University of New York Press.

Opalo, K. (2024). China as a Model Development Partner. *Africanist Perspective*. www.africanistperspective.com/p/china-as-a-model-development-partner.

Oqubay, A. (2015). *Made in Africa: Industrial Policy in Ethiopia*. Oxford: Oxford University Press.

Oqubay, A. (2019). Industrial Policy and Late Industrialization in Ethiopia. In F. Cheru, C. Cramer, & A. Oqubay (Eds.), *The Oxford Handbook of the Ethiopian Economy* (pp. 604–629). Oxford: Oxford University Press.

Oqubay, A. (2020). The Theory and Practice of Industrial Policy. In A. Oqubay, C. Cramer, H. J. Chang, & R. Kozul-Wright (Eds.), *The Oxford Handbook of Industrial Policy* (pp. 17–60). Oxford: Oxford University Press.

Oqubay, A. (2022). African Industrial Hubs and Industrialization: Diversity, Unevenness and Strategic Approach. *Transnational Corporations*, 29(1), 1–40.

Oqubay, A., & Lin, J. (Eds.) (2019). *China–Africa and an Economic Transformation*. Oxford: Oxford University Press.

Otsuka, K., Ranis, G., & Saxonhouse G. (1988). *Comparative Technology Choice in Development: The Indian and Japanese Cotton Textile Industries*. Cham: Palgrave Macmillan.

Ovadia, J. S. (2018). State-Led Industrial Development, Structural Transformation and Elite-Led Plunder: Angola (2002–2013) as a Developmental State. *Development Policy Review*, 36(5), 587–606.

Owusu, S., Tang, K., & Ndubuisi, G. (2024). *Chinese Economic Ties and Low-Carbon Industrialization in Africa*. Boston University Global Development Center. www.bu.edu/gd

Oya, C. (2019). Labour Regimes and Workplace Encounters between China and Africa. In A. Oqubay & J. Y. Lin (Eds.), *China-Africa and an Economic Transformation* (1st ed., pp. 239–262). Oxford: Oxford University Press.

Oya, C., & Schaefer, F. (2019). *Chinese Firms and Employment Dynamics in Africa: A Comparative Analysis*. IDCEA Research Report, SOAS, University of London, www.idcea.org.

Oya, C., & Schaefer, F. (2020). Industrial Hubs and the Industrial Labour Force in Africa and Asia. In Oqubay, A. & J. Y. Lin (eds.), *The Oxford Handbook of Industrial Hubs and Economic Development* (pp. 380–400). Oxford: Oxford University Press.

Oya, C., & Schaefer, F. (2021). The Politics of Labour Relations in Global Production Networks: Collective Action, Industrial Parks, and Local Conflict in the Ethiopian Apparel Sector. *World Development*, 146, 105564.

Oya, C., & Schaefer, F. (2023). Do Chinese Firms in Africa Pay Lower Wages? A Comparative Analysis of Manufacturing and Construction Firms in Angola and Ethiopia. *World Development*, 168, 106266.

Oya, C., & Schaefer, F. (2024). *ONEILO-SIRAYE Programme Ethiopia: Evaluation Report*. SOAS Global Development, Research Report No.1, London: SOAS University of London.

Oya, C., Schaefer, F., & Chen, W. (2022). *Management Workforce Localization and Skill Development in Ethiopia's Light Manufacturing*. IDCEA Research Report, SOAS, University of London. www.idcea.org

Oya. C., & Wanda, F. (2019). *Employment Patterns and Conditions in Angola: A Comparative Analysis of the Infrastructure Construction Sector and Building Materials Industry*. IDCEA Research Report, SOAS, University of London, www.idcea.org.

Page, J. (2012). Can Africa Industrialise? *Journal of African Economies*, 21 (suppl_2), ii86–ii124.

Park, Y. J., & Tang, X. (2021). Chinese FDI and Impacts on Technology Transfer, Linkages, and Learning in Africa: Evidence from the Field. *Journal of Chinese Economic and Business Studies*, 19(4), 257–268.

Pitcher, M. A. (2017). Varieties of Residential Capitalism in Africa: Urban Housing Provision in Luanda and Nairobi. *African Affairs*, 116(464), 365–390. https://doi.org/10.1093/afraf/adx009.

Pun, N., & Smith, C. (2007). Putting Transnational Labour Process in Its Place: The Dormitory Labour Regime in Post-Socialist China. *Work, Employment and Society*, 21(1), 27–45.

Qi, H., & Pringle, T. (2019). A Review of Labour Practices in China with a Focus on Construction and Garment Industries in the Context of China's 'Going out' Policy. IDCEA Working Paper n. 06. SOAS, London. https://idcea.org/wp-content/uploads/2023/10/A-Review-of-Labour-Practices-in-China-with-a-Focus-on-construction-and-garment-industries.pdf.

Qobo, M., & le Pere, G. (2018). The Role of China in Africa's Industrialization: The Challenge of Building Global Value Chains, *Journal of Contemporary China*, 27(110), 208–223.

Robertson, C. (2022). *The Time-Travelling Economist: Why Education, Electricity and Fertility Are Key to Escaping Poverty*. Cham: Springer Nature.

Rodrik, D. (2016). Premature Deindustrialization. *Journal of Economic Growth*, 21(1), 1–33.

Rodrik, D., & Sandhu, R. (2024). *Servicing Development: Productive Upgrading of Labor-Absorbing Services in Developing Economies*. Harvard University, Reimagining the Economy Policy Paper.

Rounds, Z., & Huang, H. (2017). We Are Not so Different: A Comparative Study of Employment Relations at Chinese and American Firms in Kenya. Working Paper No. 2017/10. China Africa Research Initiative, School of Advanced International Studies, Johns Hopkins University, Washington, DC.

Sautman, B., & Yan, H. (2015). *Localizing Chinese Enterprises in Africa: From Myths to Policies*. Report No. 2015–05. HKUST Institute for Emerging Market Studies.

Shen, X. (2015). Private Chinese Investment in Africa: Myths and Realities. *Development Policy Review*, 33(1), 83–106.

Shinn, D. H. (2019). China-Africa ties in historical context. In A. Oqubay & J. Y. Lin (eds.), *China-Africa and an Economic Transformation* (1st ed., pp. 61–83). Oxford: Oxford University Press.

Smith, A., Barbu, M., Campling, L., Harrison, J., & Richardson, B. (2018). Labor Regimes, Global Production Networks, and European Union Trade Policy: Labor Standards and Export Production in the Moldovan Clothing Industry. *Economic Geography*, 94(5), 550–574.

Soares De Oliveira, R. (2015). *Magnificent and beggar land: Angola since the civil war*. Oxford: Oxford University Press.

Soulé, F. (2022). Africa Can Use Great Power Rivalry to Its Benefit: Here Is How. *The Conversation*. https://theconversation.com/africa-can-use-great-power-rivalry-to-its-benefit-here-is-how-172662.

Soulé, F., Benabdallah, L., Staden, C. V., Chen, Y., & Wu, Y.-S. (2024). *Exploring the Role of Narratives in China-Africa Relations*. APRI – Africa Policy Research Private Institute gUG (haftungsbeschränkt).

Strange, A. (2023). *Chinese Global Infrastructure*. Cambridge: Cambridge University Press.

Sun, I. Y. (2017). *The Next Factory of the World: How Chinese Investment Is Reshaping Africa*. Harvard: Harvard Business Review Press.

Swider, S. (2015). *Building China: Informal Work and the New Precariat*. Ithaca: Cornell University Press.

Tang, K. (2023). The Political Economy of Special Economic Zones: The Cases of Ethiopia and Vietnam. *Review of International Political Economy*, 30(5), 1957–1983. https://doi.org/10.1080/09692290.2022.2152073.

Tang, K., Owusu, S., & Ndubuisi, G. (2024). *Chinese Investment in Africa: A Double-Edged Sword for Low-carbon Industrialization*. Global Development Policy Center. www.bu.edu/gdp/2024/07/28/chinese-investment-in-africa-a-double-edged-sword-for-low-carbon-industrialization/.

Tang, X. (2016). Does Chinese Employment Benefit Africans? Investigating Chinese Enterprises and their Operations in Africa. *African Studies Quarterly*, 16(3–4), 107–128.

Tang, X. (2018). 8 Geese Flying to Ghana? A Case Study of the Impact of Chinese Investments on Africa's Manufacturing Sector. *Journal of Contemporary China*, 27(114), 924–941.

Tang, X. (2020). *Coevolutionary Pragmatism.:Approaches and Impacts of China-Africa Cooperation*. Cambridge: Cambridge University Press.

Tang, X. (2023). China's Belt and Road Initiative and African Industrialisation. *Wenhua Zongheng. Quarterly Journal of Chinese Thought*, 1(3), 30–45.

Tang, X. (2025). China's Promotion of Knowledge Diffusion in Africa-a Case Study on Ethiopia's Manufacturing Sector. *Journal of Contemporary China*, 34(151), 145–160.

Tang, X., & Eom, J. (2019). Time Perception and Industrialization: Divergence and Convergence of Work Ethics in Chinese Enterprises in Africa. *The China Quarterly*, 238, 461–481.

Taylor, I. (2019). The Institutional Framework of Sino-African Relations. In A. Oqubay & J. Y. Lin (Eds.), *China-Africa and an Economic Transformation* (1st ed., pp. 98–126). Oxford: Oxford University Press.

Thirlwall, A. P. (2013). *Economic Growth in an Open Developing Economy: The Role of Structure and Demand*. Cheltenham: Edward Elgar.

Thompson, E. P. (1967). Time, Work-Discipline, and Industrial Capitalism. *Past & Present*, 38, 56–97.

Tregenna, F. (2023). Can Africa Run? Industrialisation and Development in Africa. *Africa Development/Afrique et Développement*, 48(2), 1–32.

Tsurumi, E. P. (1990). *Factory Girls: Women in the Thread Mills of Meiji Japan*. Princeton: Princeton University Press.

UNCTAD. (2024). *World Investment Report 2024 – Regional Trends Africa*. Geneva: UNECA.

UNECA. (2016). *Transformative Industrial Policy for Africa*. Geneva: UNECA.

UNIDO. (2024). *The Future of Industrialization*. MIPF conference. Vienna: UNIDO.

Wanda, F. (2021). *Political Capitalist Transformation: Exploring Political Elite Business Linkages in Post-War Angola*. PhD thesis, SOAS University of London.

Wanda, F., Oya, C., & Monreal, B. (2023). Building Angola: A political economy of infrastructure contractors in post-war Angola. *Journal of Southern African Studies*, 49(1), 25–47.

Wang, Y., & Zhang, H. (2024). Individual Agency in South-South Policy Transfer: China and Ethiopia's Industrial Park Development. *Review of International Political Economy*, 31(5), 1544–1568.

Wei, S. (2019). Facilitating Industrialization in Africa: China's Aid and African Industrial Capacity Building. *China Quarterly of International Strategic Studies*, 05(04), 577–599.

Wethal, U. (2018). Beyond the China Factor: Challenges to Backward Linkages in the Mozambican Construction Sector. *Journal of Modern African Studies*, 56(2), 325–351.

Whitfield, L. (2022). *Current Capabilities and Future Potential of African Textile & Apparel Value Chains: Focus on West Africa*. Centre for Business and Development Studies, Copenhagen. CBDS Working Paper No. 2022/3.

Whitfield, L., & Staritz, C. (2021). The Learning Trap in Late Industrialisation: Local Firms and Capability Building in Ethiopia's Apparel Export Industry. *The Journal of Development Studies*, 57(6), 980–1000.

Whitfield, L., & Zalk, N. (2020). Phases and Uneven Experiences in African Industrial Policy. In A. Oqubay, C. Cramer, H.-J. Chang, & R. Kozul-Wright (Eds.), *The Oxford Handbook of Industrial Policy* (pp. 841–866). Oxford: Oxford University Press.

Wolf, C. (2016). China and Latecomer Industrialization Processes in Sub-Saharan Africa: A Case of Combined and Uneven Development. *World Review of Political Economy*, 7(2), 249–284.

Wolf, C. (2017). Industrialization in Times of China: Domestic-Market Formation in Angola. *African Affairs*, 116(464), 435–461.

Wolf, C. (2024). Construction as a Springboard for Industrialisation: Chinese Overseas Construction Projects and Structural Transformation in Angola, Ethiopia and Nigeria. *The European Journal of Development Research*, 36 (3), 639–667.

World Bank. (2012). *Chinese FDI in Ethiopia: A World Bank Survey*. Washington, DC: World Bank.

World Bank. (2016). *Why so Idle? Wages and Employment in a Crowded Labor Market*. Ethiopia 5th Economic Update, Washington, DC: World Bank.

World Bank. (2021). *Industrialization in Sub-Saharan Africa: Seizing Opportunities in Global Value Chains*. Washington, DC: World Bank.

Wu, T. (2024). The Political Economy of Variations in Energy Debt Financing by Two Chinese Policy Banks in Africa. *Development and Change*, 55(6), 1259–1288.

Xia, Y. (2021). Chinese Investment in East Africa: History, Status, and Impacts. *Journal of Chinese Economic and Business Studies*, 19(4), 269–293.

Xu, L. (2022). Engendering China – Africa Encounters: Chinese Family Firms, Black Women Workers and the Gendered Politics of Production in South Africa. *The China Quarterly*, 250, 356–375.

Xu, L. (2024). From 'Made in China' to 'Made in Africa'? *Foro*. www.revistaforo.com/2024/0803-01-EN.

Yimer, A., & Geda, A. (2024). A Two-Edged Sword: The Impact of Public Debt on Economic Growth – the Case of Ethiopia. *Journal of Applied Economics*, 27(1), 2398908.

Young, A. A. (1928). Increasing Returns and Econ Progress. *Economic Journal*, 38, 527–542.

Yu, Y. (2024). Africa, China, and the Race for Critical Minerals: A New Focus for FOCAC? *The Diplomat*. https://thediplomat.com/2024/08/africa-china-and-the-race-for-critical-minerals-a-new-focus-for-focac/.

Zhang, H. (2021). *Chinese International Contractors in Africa: Structure and Agency*. Working Paper No. 2021/47. China Africa Research Initiative, School of Advanced International Studies, Johns Hopkins University, Washington, DC. www.sais-cari.org/publications.

Zhang, H. (2023). *From Contractors to Investors? Evolving Engagement of Chinese State Capital in Global Infrastructure Development and the Case of Lekki Port in Nigeria*. Working Paper No. 2023/53. China Africa Research Initiative, School of Advanced International Studies, Johns Hopkins University, Washington, DC. www.sais-cari.org/publications.

Zhao, Z. Y., & Shen, L. Y. (2008). Are Chinese Contractors Competitive in International Markets? *Construction Management and Economics*, 26(3), 225–236.

Zhou, H. (2022). Western and Chinese Development Engagements in Uganda's Roads Sector: An Implicit Division of Labour. *African Affairs*, 121(482), 29–59.

Zhou, J. (2023). How Can China Contribute to the Continent's Economic Development? *Wenhua Zongheng. Quarterly Journal of Chinese Thought*, 1(3), 13–29.

Acknowledgments

The research on which this Element is based was supported by the DFID-ESRC Growth Research Programme (DEGRP) (Grant numbers: ESRC ES/M004228/1 and ES/T001933/1). This research would not have been possible without the various contributions to the research process as acknowledged in Oya and Schaefer (2019). This Element's manuscript benefitted from very useful comments from two anonymous reviewers and the editor of the Series. Arkebe Oqubay and Chris Cramer also contributed with very insightful comments. Ken Barlow provided exceptional professional editorial assistance. Robert Ertel, Matthew Li, and Thabo Huntgeburth contributed with valuable research assistance. I presented the main arguments of the Element to audiences for feedback and reactions at Peking University in 2024, the New School for Social Research in 2023, Hong Kong University of Science and Technology in 2021, the Development Studies Association conferences in 2020 and 2021, the Ethiopian Investment Commission national labour workshop (2023), the European Conference of African Studies in 2023, and the International Initiative for Promoting Political Economy conference in 2023. Many of the insights in this Element were shaped by conversations with countless workers, company managers, government officials and other key informants who engaged with our probing questions over several years. My co-researchers Florian Schaefer and Weiwei Chen have been a great source of comradeship and inspiration since we started this exciting research journey together in 2015. Qi Hao, Tang Xiaoyang, Christina Wolf, Dic Lo, Fekadu Nigussie, Borja Monreal and Fernandes Wanda also contributed to some of this thinking and evidence during this process. Thank you to Ching Kwan Lee for excellent editorial guidance, and especially for persuading me to take on this challenge and offering unrelenting encouragement. Finally, I dedicate this Element to my family for their steady support, love, and inspiration.

Global China

Ching Kwan Lee
University of California-Los Angeles

Ching Kwan Lee is professor of sociology at the University of California-Los Angeles. Her scholarly interests include political sociology, popular protests, labor, development, political economy, comparative ethnography, China, Hong Kong, East Asia and the Global South. She is the author of three multiple award-winning monographs on contemporary China: Gender and the South China Miracle: Two Worlds of Factory Women (1998), Against the Law: Labor Protests in China's Rustbelt and Sunbelt (2007), and The Specter of Global China: Politics, Labor and Foreign Investment in Africa (2017). Her co-edited volumes include Take Back Our Future: an Eventful Sociology of Hong Kong's Umbrella Movement (2019) and The Social Question in the 21st Century: A Global View (2019).

About the Series

The Cambridge Elements series Global China showcases thematic, region- or country-specific studies on China's multifaceted global engagements and impacts. Each title, written by a leading scholar of the subject matter at hand, combines a succinct, comprehensive and up-to-date overview of the debates in the scholarly literature with original analysis and a clear argument. Featuring cutting edge scholarship on arguably one of the most important and controversial developments in the 21st century, the Global China Elements series will advance a new direction of China scholarship that expands China Studies beyond China's territorial boundaries.

Cambridge Elements

Global China

Elements in the Series

Chinese Soft Power
Maria Repnikova

Clash of Empires: From 'Chimerica' to the 'New Cold War'
Ho-fung Hung

The Hong Kong-China Nexus: A Brief History
John Carroll

Global China as Method
Ivan Franceschini and Nicholas Loubere

Hong Kong: Global China's Restive Frontier
Ching Kwan Lee

China and Global Food Security
Shaohua Zhan

China in Global Health: Past and Present
Mary Augusta Brazelton

Chinese Global Infrastructure
Austin Strange

Global China's Shadow Exchange
Tak-Wing Ngo

Global Civil Society and China
Anthony J. Spires

China and the Global Economic Order
Gregory T Chin and Kevin P. Gallagher

China for Africa's Industrialization?
Carlos Oya

A full series listing is available at: www.cambridge.org/EGLC

For EU product safety concerns, contact us at Calle de José Abascal, 56–1°, 28003 Madrid, Spain or eugpsr@cambridge.org.

www.ingramcontent.com/pod-product-compliance
Lightning Source LLC
LaVergne TN
LVHW011849060526
838200LV00054B/4242